Publisher's Note: We regret that the last four stanzas of Kelly Cherry's "On Watching a Young Man Play Tennis" (page 30) were inadvertently omitted. The complete poem follows.

On Watching a Young Man Play Tennis

The male poets run, lifting their feet like pros.
Others fish, and then there are those
Whose driving force
Sends them to the sandtraps of an eighteen-hole course

In search of metaphor. I have no yen
For sun and sky and earth, no kin-
Ship for the sea.
The element of mind is quite enough for me,

And dreaming in the damp of poolside shade,
I let imagination wade
Through the shallow
Stretch of time beyond a bend of tanning elbow,

And burning thigh, to where the poet plays
A love game with my yesterdays.
I have no zest
For exercise, no yearning after limberness

For the sake of limb alone, but enjoy,
Girlishly, this energy of Boy
That seeks to know
The meaning of *mens sana in corpore sano.*

Turning on my side, I see the shadow
Of his racket on the court grow
Long and widen
Till its very silence trespasses on the Haydn

Which carries from the house, and I put down
My drink and move inside where sound
And light and drift
Of dinner's smells serve, albeit fleetingly, to lift

My spirits to a plane of praise upon
Which I can stand and frankly own
That I am tired,
And lazy, and will leave to others more inspired

The satisfaction of the outdoor sports.
A young man in his tennis shorts
Suffices to
Realign the balance of my brain and back so

That I am paralyzed with memory
Of verse and versifier. (Yet I
Remember when
I volleyed more than words with the artfullest of men.)

UNCOMMONPLACE

UNCOMMONPLACE

An Anthology of
Contemporary Louisiana Poets

EDITED BY

ANN BREWSTER DOBIE

LOUISIANA STATE UNIVERSITY PRESS   BATON ROUGE

1998

Copyright © 1998 by Louisiana State University Press
All rights reserved
Manufactured in the United States of America
First printing
07 06 05 04 03 02 01 00 99 98   5 4 3 2 1

Designer: Laura Roubique Gleason
Typeface: Palatino, with Serlio display
Typesetter: Wilsted & Taylor Publishing Services
Printer and binder: Thomson-Shore, Inc.

Library of Congress Cataloging-in-Publication Data
Uncommonplace : an anthology of contemporary Louisiana poets / edited
    by Ann Brewster Dobie.
        p.   cm.
    ISBN 0–8071–2254–8 (alk. paper).—ISBN 0–8071–2255–6 (pbk. :
alk. paper)
        1. American poetry—Louisiana.   2. American poetry—20th century.
    3. Louisiana—Poetry.   I. Dobie, Ann B.
    PS558.L8U53   1998
    811'.54'0809763—dc21   97–46685
                                                                CIP

The paper in this book meets the guidelines for permanence and durability
of the Committee on Production Guidelines for Book Longevity of the
Council on Library Resources. ♾

CONTENTS

Contents

Contents

Contents

Contents

Contents

Contents

Contents

PREFACE

Robert Graves, himself a poet of some renown, has been quoted as saying that "to be a poet is a condition rather than a profession." He might have been speaking of the poets in this volume, for few of them make their living exclusively through their writing. In completing a form that asks them to name their occupation, they would be more likely to write "professor" or "grandmother," "petroleum landman" or "insurance salesman," than "poet." But they know the importance of what they do when they write. Each is drawn to experimenting with words as a means of re-creating the lives they live and the worlds they observe. Through images, sounds, and forms they set down experience as it occurs to them, moving emotion and thought through the imagination until they find a way to say more than the words mean. They are poets.

More particularly, they are Louisiana poets, even if some of them now live here more in memory than in fact. When, with support from the Louisiana Division of the Arts and the Louisiana Endowment for the Humanities, Louisianians were invited to submit their poems for possible publication in this anthology of works by currently active writers, the poems came not only from cities, villages, and farms throughout the state, but from states spread across the map, from Maine to Washington, where, despite time and distance, some poets continue to think of themselves as belonging to the towns and fields and bayous where they once lived. As varied in subject and style as the many cultures that make up Louisiana, the submissions bore rich testimony to the talent produced and nurtured here. They came, written with varying degrees of expertise, in French and English, from black and white, by young people and old, in their very numbers bearing evidence of the long Louisiana tradition of attempting to understand experience by transforming it into story and song. In an age rarely described as "poetic," Louisiana poets prove to be alive, abundant, and active.

How were the poems collected here chosen from the many submitted? Initially, a panel of readers considered each one, moving toward selection of the strongest by individual reading, joint discussion, rereading, and more discussion. That first selection was followed by three others due to the panel's desire to include more of the poets and works that deserve public notice. In the end, the voices of sixty-seven writers have been gathered in this volume. Individually they express concern and care for the past and present, for the personal and social. Each offers the reader the pleasures of recognition and surprise. But it is perhaps as a group that they have the most significance, for together they represent a rich natural resource often overlooked by Louisianians. They represent the creative spirit of those who have dwelled here.

Several years in the making, this project owes its progress and completion to the active interest of many people and several groups. I am grateful to all those who lent their help and need to single out some of the most generous among them.

From the beginning Tom Boozer, then Director of the Acadiana Arts Council, Derek Gordon, formerly Director of the Louisiana Division of the Arts, and Michael Sartisky, Executive Director of the Louisiana Endowment for the Humanities, recognized the importance of providing a way for currently active Louisiana writers—storytellers and poets—to be heard. With their help, the project received initial financial assistance from the Louisiana Division of the Arts and the Louisiana Endowment for the Humanities. I am grateful for the early affirmation from these men, which gave me the encouragement to begin and, in the long run, to continue.

The first stage of the project came to fruition in 1991 with the publication of *Something in Common: Contemporary Louisiana Stories*. Although poetry was not included in that volume, many of the poems that appear in this one were reviewed by the panel of readers who studied the many manuscripts submitted for the earlier book. Thus, my thanks go once again to Delores Harbuck of Shreveport, John Wood of McNeese State University, and Timothy Gautreaux of Southeastern Louisiana University, who drew on their reading experience and expertise to study the many submitted poems and to make their respective recommendations.

Since the contents of the present volume took shape, the project has stayed alive due to the efforts of many people, not least among them Margaret Dalrymple, former editor in chief, and John Easterly, executive editor, at Louisiana State University Press. To Bruce Dobie, too, I owe a debt of gratitude for first entertaining the idea to collect the works of active Louisiana writers and refusing to let it go.

Uncommonplace

Ralph Adamo

It'll Never Be Warm Again

The brown prairie in the icy dawn.
Stiff grasses and a cold sun and the wind
So dry it's hard to breathe it in. Yeah,
that'd be nice.
And there's James Wright bowed in his window.
Furrowed broken lonely
he listens,
the hiss of the flame in close confines.
He's had more love than most.

Once in the Lacquered Afterform of the Dream

Giny had a dog named Jeremy, a dog
so low and thick his voicings poured
out of him like moon tit milk,
and when they'd come to visit our house,
that moored vessel where death's four
first mates fiddled skipperless from
dusk to dusk, this happened: a pint
of light appeared in all our hands
and we quaffed that light and felt
ourselves at sea, she was that
entertaining, while Jeremy in the kitchen
rustled bones from our cracker-
jack garbage collection.

Old Numbers

Old magazines I can't open
for fear of finding something
beautiful—a story—unresolved,

forgotten, or just a whole idea
nobody's heard in fifty years,
even though it was a good one.

The artists with their models,
the writers about whom no stories
are told, the eyestrain of the thing,
the way the dank smell seems
specific to the act of opening
one page from the next, releasing
some pressure from a deep earthly
sleep, not of rot but music
like flying bugs mad for a dead
tree. Those old magazines,
they sit there, like ambition
caught in the war, frozen.

Azaleas

Sisters climb the bedroom window, lay themselves on the night table like pink fish, like negligees and soap slivers, diaphanous, pale veined. Wrapped through doors, leopard-spotted nectar paths pour down a wash of purple stars. I remember women in New Orleans, some driven through humid hours like orchids in a cooler, and others all azalea, wild pink shrubs that trumpeted in hot places, flagrant and profuse. Night came on so strong there, the smear of color and funereal perfume, every bloom corpulent on flood and rain. My friend and I walked the Quarter eating butter pastry and oysters. Six feet tall, she glowed against the courtyard Venus, a marble goddess who tasted the world's saliva as if it were champagne. Sax men poured tunes like hot cane, just to make my friend laugh. When Venus danced, flowers opened. Freaks spun round her like multicolored ribbons. As if she groomed her handsome children, my friend embraced men with faces shaped like figs. She kept a pond for beasts behind a black iron fence, behind the Quarter on Lessups Street, and a gravestone in the grass. Near dawn I slept on her guest bed, sweating against red satin, while a silver fan clacked overhead. Sun cut through leaded windows, spun the air to hot glass. Black coffee with thick cream, huge strawberries in a mahogany dining room. We hid from the heat and talked of dying—the flickering boats our fathers rode to the spirit world, the little hulls of morphine. As the air began to wave and drip, we walked the streets again, both dressed in white gauze with crisp straw hats, then wispy, drooping damp. We headed for her levee shack, three lilting rooms of bird nests. Water, the dissolving river, lapped the back porch, the pilings. *Tell me about a lover,* she'd say, causing a lip of wine to sing under her index finger. We never touched, but in the tuberous wave of our voices, we drifted for days. As I drove north one dark, past St. Charles and into the bayou, a rainstorm changed the livid horizon to brown, then bruise. How sweet azaleas at the beginning, breathing in the swamps, breathing in the streets, their fuschia bodies covering our feet. How brief our beauty in sugared heat—our dresses lifted and fell those hours between the wicker and dying rafters like opulent clouds of steam.

Pole Boat at Honey Island

The way he pushes deeper
into everything I hate—the heat rising
like wet crepe from silt and muck
to fill our lungs with its rotten breath.

Listen to the grunting armadillos
pad the tule pond on tiny feet.
Listen to the owl croon
in the loblolly.

I want to be brave, to bathe
myself in the humid night,
to cross the irradiant lawn
under magnolias,

those creamy-faced babies
perched in evergreen leaves,
to float through dives,
sick-smelling bayous full of turtle,

yellow-capped night heron,
to let the air penetrate at last, the miasma
that sends women to attics, sets them scratching walls
like mice, rocking, humming with no release.

But I am afraid. I have danced
the sad slippers. I have placed
a hand on blind branches,
felt it flame with fire ants.

My lover's body like watersnakes,
his sweat the odor of crawfish,
boiled. As he poles deeper
into the gauzy night—

the water swims with kerosene.
So too as peepers fill
their bugle pouches—
like voices in an asylum,

an orchestra of cracked reeds,
throbbing sacs of chameleon—
we strum our giddy throats.
We begin to screech.

On the Veranda We Drink Gin and Tonic

The elephant ears
tired of hearing witty stories
twist flat on their stems.
The flashy camellias drop to the lawn
like abandoned prom dresses. In Baton Rouge,
the falling over begins. Unmindful,
we might dissolve like aspirin
in the moist night air.

If it's not the falling over,
it's the standing up.
The bartender keeps a battalion of rags
in white uniform. I've seen him
beat a peacock rug to bloody red.
Isn't that how the cubists began,
separating the white threads of canvas
into a field of broken glass?

Nature *morte:* shaping the guitar
from wood-grained paper,
laying it flat so that one might embrace
every side at once.
Three women lean on their elbows
like collapsing tripods,
and see how their malaise fractures
into radiant blue prisms?

With a moment's stay against geometry
this landscape could turn suddenly impolite.

We might break each other open
like the clear pink coat of a shrimp.
Perhaps we'd become friends,
the way cartoonists drew Frankenstein's scars
with zippers, as if anyone could
enter his curious skin.

Suite du loup, no. je ne sais plus

Le loup rode la nuit sans lune
A deux pattes pour éviter
De se laisser avoir, pour éviter
De laisser savoir la faim
De son histoire sans fin,
Sans dénouement.
A la pleine lune il reprendra
Ses griffes pour courir
Les bois. Pour le moment il parcourt
Les bars, hurlant au néon.
Il déchire les symboles aux yeux bleus
Entre les dents de son imagination.
Il fait semblant de rire
Derrière son masque d'homme,
Amarrant son coeur
Jusqu'au sang prochain.

Ouragan III

Un enfant est arraché de son père
Qui essayait de tenir sa petite main dans la sienne,
Et qui lui disait que ça allait tout finir bien.
Il comprend pas tout de suite
Qu'il va jamais le revoir encore.
Les événements le ramassent
Et l'amène dans le trou noir
Derrière la raison.
Le tourbillon engendré par le vide
Dans son milieu
Cache tout assez longtemps
Pour perdre le garçon.
Ça se passe si vite qu'on se demande pas

Ayoù il a passé jusqu'à quelques moments
Après l'arrivée de la pluie.
Debout au milieu du rien qui reste
Avec les clous qui tombent du ciel violet.
Le père se trouve chanceux d'être là,
De sentir la peur et le froid dans les veines,
De sentir les narines qui essaient de haler assez d'air
Pour fournir au cœur qui veut exploser,
A la tête qui essaie de nager à travers du vertige,
Aux oreilles qui cherchent un son essentiel dans le silence
Et aux yeux qui brûlent pour voir au-delà du dégat,
Et c'est là, à ce moment imprécis,
Qu'il aperçoit l'absence.
Et son premier regret est
Que ses dernières paroles à son fils
Etaient une menterie.

JACK B. BEDELL

In the Marsh

I followed my father past the camp,
past the two pecan trees
and the pine that marked our boundary,
black mud sucking my hip boots
as I ran behind him.

When we reached the bayou
I froze in the marsh grass
at a black-tailed deer
collapsed into the bank,
skin draped like linen
over the hoops of its ribs.

Its nose still dipped into the water;
its stomach swelled.
Around it the marsh hovered,
swirled; insects dived and crawled,
hurried to hide the body.

I wanted to hurry, too,
but the deer's stillness kept me
from bolting. I held my ears
against the humming of blue flies
and pressed into my father's shirt.
He shrugged over me, ready to fish,
pulled me away from the deer's empty sockets.
I forced myself not to look,
not to see the deer disappear,
not to watch the beetles
dig into the deer's stale flesh.

Death, my father explained,
and slapped my back as if to pat it in.
I cast harder and more often
until I could look at him

and no longer see his eyes
fall back into their sockets,
until I could ignore his hollow hand
patting me on the shoulders,
until his words faded into the marsh's breathing.

The Maker in the Sky

Driving north toward you
over spillways and marshes
I lose myself to highway lines
and am pulled from the world
of road signs and rest stops.
Warning marks under my tires
become enemy fire
blasting into my cockpit.
Gauge needles pop left
and I pull the lever to float
free of the wreckage.

Dangling safely on the air
I am the maker in the sky.
The smoke from my dying Corsair
wraps around me, red ducks vee by
and I conduct their passing.
I shape the rising land
into colored squares and textures
and find a place to hover down—
no magic ocean filled with sharks
but a marsh very much like home
with warm, brown water
and reeds to swallow me.

I lie on my back, wet to the ears
and survey the sky I've made,

clouds and birds circling, blue
holding all above me,
as my parachute falls
like a wedding dress
over a rising cypress tree.

Sleeping with the Net-Maker

She speaks to me when she's asleep.
Her lips move but do not mean
anything against the dark,
each word air on my fingertips,
each breath a twitch in her chest.
At night I am another boundary
containing her in her sleep
like the blue linen ducks flying
beneath her spreading hair, the sheets
twisting between her glowing legs,
the wooden frame holding her
above the cold wooden floor.
I watch her when she cannot know.

Tonight I watch her hands weave
a winding net over us.
They float above the lines of her stomach
tying each knot and squaring it off
until the room is filled with twine.

Soon she'll be the fisherman
seining air for loaves of fish.
She casts her net with arms spread out,
feet together, hair swirling.
Outside the water cracks
against the glass to catch
her throw. It gives up its form

to take her net and washes over
into the room teeming with fish
and bread, thick with what she wants.

I watch her cast for hours and learn
to live beneath her gray water.
She spills redfish at my feet
but I tell her I'm not hungry.
Her lips still move for me as she pulls
the net toward us. I lie down
among her piles of bread.

A Song

The opening mouth,
                    a stone under water,
a skiff poised in the bruised stillness of oars.

The voice,
                    ice cracking in warm water,
the flutter of wings startled into flight.

The lyrics,
                    words trembling, boiling water,
a man in the distance walking on gravel.

The music,
                    to the eyes, falling water,
to the hands, a rope unraveling into strands.

The final chord,
                    a wall of water,
already dead, a man about to fall.

The silence after song,
                        the hard edge of water,
glaciers advancing on the cities.

A Short History of Barbed Wire

I have seen strands of it float like spittle
drooling from a swollen tongue.
And the whimpering body snared in its tiny claws
reminded me of someone singing into a harmonica.

I have seen a bald girl jerk away her hand
as from a vine of thorns—a delicate pink flower
cupped in her palm, jagged petals of flesh
curling back from the wound.

I have heard it in the wind, teeth without a mouth,
and behind it a million mouths without teeth,
a million mouths that turn to us with the same face:
small-boned, polite, and full of forgiveness.

Sestina

The rain was coming down.
We were in bed.
The moon came through the window.
One of us was in tears.
The floors were cold.
We stayed where we were.

The rain stayed where it was.
We were coming down.
We were cold.
The floors were in bed.
The moon was in tears.
One of us came through the window.

The rain came through the window.
One of us stayed where he was.
We were in tears.
The moon was coming down.
We were in bed.
The floors were cold.

The rain was cold.
The floors came through the window.
One of us was in bed.
We stayed where we were.
We were coming down.
The moon was in tears.

The rain was in tears.
The moon was cold.
The floors were coming down.
We came through the window.
One of us stayed where he was.
We were in bed.

The rain was in bed.
We were in tears.
The moon stayed where it was.
One of us was cold.
The floors came through the window.
We were coming down.

DARRELL BOURQUE

Le Courir de Mardi Gras

Early in the morning all the men
of the *grand courir* line up
behind our leader, dressed in passion's
red. In cone and cape, looking like
a lost marauder of another time,
he takes us through the countryside
where we dismount at every house,
raising clouds of dust. Beating out
the tune. It is all triangle ring
and squeeze-box strain. Sometimes,
even early in the day, we take our
brothers in our arms as we sing and
dance, forgetting we wear masks.
We get caught up in the act. We are
fire and air. We will not remember
until tomorrow our separateness,
and that we are also earth.

Holy Water

1

We must begin
with what we have
at hand.

Your mother is water.
You are water.
She runs Tigris
and Euphrates
through your veins.

Her Nile flows
into the waters
of your longest river.

Rivers she gives
are not gifts.
They never separate
themselves enough
from the two of you for that.

She will give you a drum river.
It will beat over you
sleeping in the high branches
in a sling she made
just for you.

One day you will fall
suddenly.
The fall will force you open.

You will hit the skin
of the drumhead yourself
for the first time,
and it will change
everything.

You will be music
from that moment.
Everything else you do
will be accompaniment.
You are a sacramental,
a thrumming. You are
making all of time
a vigil.

She will give you a river
to teach you the mountains
in you, your jungles,

the dense green foliage,
how you will have to breathe
all those different airs.
Vines in you and all
those leaves
like large green sails.

The piranha, the pirarucu,
the crocodile, and the dolphin
swim in this river.
Overhead in currents of palpable
green air parrots voice
various tongues. Macaws
scream and toucans yelp
like packs of dogs.

Some rivers she will give you
to show you the rightness
of naming things as they are.
These you might call great river,
or long river. In one of these
you will learn to love long
golden necklaces laughing
like unattended children
in school yards. In another
you will learn flat, slow,
and opaque, and love them, too.
You will be taught swift currents.
You will meet the seducer in you
who wants you in other riverbeds.

In some places these rivers will be called
Congo and Amazon, Yangtze or Ch'ang Chiang.
In some these rivers will be called
Mississippi and Atchafalaya.
But you will not call them by those names.

This, she is telling you, is no atlas
you are living in.

These rivers she gives you
so you will know her when you see her.
These rivers she gives you
so you will feel her pushing against you
when you hear your names.

2

My oldest daughter's first drawing,
a fish with glasses. It slips into a white sea
under her hands.
When we see it, it swims head on
past the undercolor of white on white. Blood
red, it waves

its exaggerated fins. It holds itself
in both the first and last water it will swim in. The same
color as the fish,
this water closest to us, a network
of horizontal lines clearly put on last. They waver so,
it is difficult to tell

how many there are. They mark some river
or some sea the fish will go to. Some water boundary
stopping it. Or something
holding it. The nearsighted fish
is happy, its fins shifting as it slow-dances,
wide-eyed, between there and here.

3

Australian aborigines stopped
from time to time in their wanderings
from one place to another. They stopped,

they said, to let catch up to them
what we might call their spirits, the spirit
being the slower swimmer sometimes,
loving the warm waters of whatever river
it has gotten used to floating in.

My father in his father's
field, my uncle in his father's. The old men
who moved from one piece of land to another,
I have seen them, stopped for a time,
on the head rows in the middle of the field,
just waiting until something makes them go
again.

My grandmother in the middle
of her yard, each palm turned away from the hip
it rests upon, each hand a small pink butterfly
just lighting for a while.

The ancients knew this stopping well.
They gave their poets chairs by the water to sit in.
These water watchers told their people of all the rivers
they could see from there, of all the rivers they could dream.
The low drones in them, the tearing sounds of water over gravel
it has loosened, the limpid sounds of happy, noisy children
playing, those sounds you have to train your ears to even begin
to hear. The high twittering, the low drag, both slipping
always from the bag of sound. All those sounds
the poets will make their words with.

Their best words, the ones making sounds
already in the water you swim in. Their best words,
the ones with river sounds you can only hear
when they say them and your eyes water. Small floodings
in the heart when you see yourself for the first time,
the body going momentarily to its source.

You see yourself in the fishes in the rivers
they see and hear, in the rivers they name and call you to
and hold you in. It is in that water you might say that you see
God and thrash about so that you can come up to say it,
or you might just feel something swimming into you,
something lighter than anything you have ever known
swimming past the boundary you think your flesh is.
You will hold this penetration in you,
there being no word you know yet for this interlocking
so far inside you that you will have to make new charts
for a new world extending farther than you ever could have known.

The Grammar of Verbenas

I am turning from my mother. I am moving
to the person with the camera perhaps,
a single verbena blossom in my right hand.
The date on the Fox snapshot tells me now
I am six. I am turning or being turned
by it, a flame I am holding to someone
higher, a flame I am ready to offer
to someone bigger than I am. Others
are in the shot, two sisters, an aunt,
little more than a child herself
looking off into the distance. Granny,
my great-grandmother, always turned
her face to the side when she knew
her image was being made. She was there.
Looking off into another distance,
her nose almost touching her chin.
We used to say when she took out her teeth
she could have brought them together
if she could have been persuaded to try.

But I don't think it was any of these
people in the picture.
                                   I think it was
someone outside the field who said something
that put weight and form into the flower.
It was like that moment you are with others,
and no one has had to say anything, clearly
you are all just passing time. You look up
or to the side too soon to see accounts
are being taken. You will not be there
at the inventory or the disputation.
Your advocate will be weak or mildly
disinterested.
                          You were going on, they say,
about flowers and what they are and when.
You were going on about nitrogen and how
it is necessary for all life, about how
one moment air is just air, the next,
flower, stem, and root, this gas three parts
of all air we breathe, oxygen the other part,
its chemical symbol N, its atomic number
7. Some of this, especially the latter,
was in your head but you are certain
it was never part of what you said
to them. How this lighter than air gas
is the essential part of the green
in stem and leaf. You said that.
You were going on about splayed iron
burning in the petals, going on
about filigreed blood, blood fountains,
burnt water at the end of your hand.
Burnt water, you remember telling them that,
feeling something catch then, and you know
you are part of another story
and you will not be the teller of it.

But you go on. Turning to each of them
in some formality of generosity
you carry on so they won't be the ones
embarrassed.
                              You go on about flower
before it is flower, certainly before
it is something like verbena. You bring
your talk back to one burnt water flowing
into another burnt water, your hand
and the flower it must hold, then give away.
You tell them that it is this turning
that turns us. In your head another story
unfolds. They are telling you what you hold
is flower, a rather common one at that
in these parts, in no way starting point
for the revolution you have in mind.
There is enough here for everyone
is the appropriate response but a leap
in the talk closes the opening where
what could have been said is just lining up
as some sayable.
                              Something like that
perhaps. Something almost said perhaps that
somehow gets itself to you, catches you
in midstride like the flash in the audience
the announcer warns about the danger of,
the blinding light going off in the dark,
in the legs, in the solar plexus, changing
all that air. In the quickness of it,
impossible to tell what senses what.
It is something perhaps as far removed
from a boy being turned by a flower as
the nutty, earth smell his father was,
but still you can bring that something
to your nerve endings daily. You can bring

it to yourself as easily as the light, clear
yellow, something like a high, clear sound
that is your lover's scent mixed with all that
sharp green air.
                    One moment you are the dancer
stretched into air, yours to move on, to hang
above. And then it is air gone simply air.
You see in that instant what it all looks like
from the house. How transparent the floor feels
even now. You are not at all sure the flash came
before the crack. You do not know what broke.
You are not even sure you're not still moving
as the curtain swings shut so near your head.
It was something like that.
                    For years you
will prepare brilliant defenses. You will
turn to history. You will study cartography.
You will speak in tongues. *Florida,*
Florianopolis, the *Flores Sea, Firenze,*
Florentia, Florence; bhel 3: Indo-European
root meaning to thrive, blossom. Probably
from *bhel-2:* to blow, swell with derivatives
referring to various round objects and to
the notion of tumescent masculinity; *blowan,*
florescence, folium, phullon, blom; wer-3:
base of various Indo-European roots;
to turn, bend; *werthan,* to become;
flos, blostma, florin, bladaz, blaed,
bloma, bloom, blossom, *wordam* / word,
verbum / word, verbena, blossom, *blom.*

Oysters

These bodies!—given to their different
hungers—mine for yours, with or without
such aphrodisiacs as these; and always
too the voice of Messer Gaster clamoring
for satisfaction. Here in a hemisphere
of shell, all rough and rococo, we find
a store of pleasure, bathing in a nacred

pool of brine—a sensuous tongue to meet
our tongue, to which we add the piquancy
of lemon and a pepper sauce. Oh virtue
in consuming what we love! What, however,
of the oyster's own affairs—its business
beneath a bank of sea grasses—attending
to the currents, or perhaps a pearl? All

comes to nothing now, because its small
and slippery body, lost to feeling, fits
so well my own, which can devour a dozen
more, with wine, sustaining in delight
its purposes . . . and then that other need,
which we have not forgotten—our desire,
enhanced by your cologne, my décolleté,

kisses as apéritif, these tasty morsels
for the palate, and mostly by the salt
of passing time. An oyster world awaits
us, like the tender forms of creatures,
like our own, a hostage to its appetites,
which are its possibilities—in ecstasy,
the taking and the making of this flesh.

New Orleans: The Winter Hour

In half-rain, half-sleet, the sycamores
and hackberry trees, reduced
to bones, have given up their illusions—
a proscenium torn at the back,
showing the winter side of the Garden
District—not just the usual steeples,
but houses, down to the glaze
of kitchen windows, the dejection

of dripping brick, and walls as grey
as washing that will not dry;
then the wary eyes of McGehee's School,
a paste façade on Jackson Avenue,
and, beyond, remnants of the Eiffel Tower
restaurant, shipped to New Orleans
for some entrepreneur's grand schemes—
with the twinned tinsel bridges

hanging over the spires and the river—
pinning together east and west
in a cold embrace. I am losing the lines
of force that hold together
the quotidian—curtains of trees,
vectors of sky and gable; and the aporias
of the dying year resist
all grasp—more a hollow in feeling

than thought itself—an emptiness,
with barely a word to haul it in. The rain
lies down over my mind.
How time reveals us, darkly, to ourselves!
The city is alive, even in its winter
throes, but my old friend,
having rounded his last December,
has just shot himself in the mouth.

Tulips

In winter, flowers in the window, mauve
and cream and deep vermilion, heralding
a mildness riding in with March, while winds
deny it—tulips, amaryllis, palms
in pots, as from some island of the mind
assuming shape. Now in a mute surprise,

and crackling crystal paper, tulips flame,
a royal apparition mingling leaves
and stems with globes of oriental light.
A green remembrance overflows the room,
as in an armload and arranged in glass
they turn the season. What *hauteur,* what sleek

distinction in their raiment! To be grained
and silkened with inimitable hue
induces metaphysics of the eye—
conspiring beyond voluted lines,
as if a noble, long-stemmed nonchalance
were not the end, the very end, of thought.

Programming an Evening Away from Home

Thieves' music is music for an intruder's ear.
I choose these bars instead of burglar guards.
You scurry past alarms through a barrage
of hammers striking deftly outworn felts
or leap through purging fire of twin guitars.
I lock my door with keys of string quartets
as my cat eyes me curiously from the edge
of his most recent pedestal. Pure pet,
he composes himself to each new accompaniment.
Come rapist, murderer. Come privateer;
your score is here. Move heirlooms out by stealth.
In ballet mime now pillage clef by clef
each golden moment from knickknack shelf;
then tie the loot with a frayed extension cord
that would form your noose from one coloratura's word.

Dance of the Wino in Lafayette Square

Faltering in battered felt,
he moves in a breeze of fermenting breath
and the girl without a partner
who dances under the trees
casts her shadow
that weaves as he weaves—
an outline on the ground
where pigeons feed on seeds of silhouettes.

She sees she is not seen.
Those eyes that once could hold a world of green
now overflow their lids with muscatel.
Chiaroscuros climb the monument
in time to distant woodwinds, nearer brass.
No shadow falls or stumbles in this grass,

but is fluid in each movement
while branches ripple in the place of bone
and slept-in clothes are ironed by the sun
so elegantly black, they will forsake
the body soon—and shadows dance alone.

Homecoming

The glass knob comes off in your hand
while your key is in the lock.
Brass might do the same
if you are thinking that this substance
has betrayed you.
It has not. Too much wrenching
of a world taken for granted
will tell you things fall apart unexpectedly.
Something loosens quietly inside,
gives way without warning
to leave you on this steaming pavement—
barred from any sanctuary.
A glass eye enlarger looks out through
                the peephole,
freezes you to the spot
on the threshold of your own chilled
                interior
as you turn on your palm
a crystal of burning ice.

On Watching a Young Man Play Tennis

The male poets run, lifting their feet like pros.
Others fish, and then there are those
Whose driving force
Sends them to the sandtraps of an eighteen-hole course

In search of metaphor. I have no yen
For sun and sky and earth, no kin-
Ship for the sea.
The element of mind is quite enough for me,

And dreaming in the damp of poolside shade,
I let imagination wade
Through the shallow
Stretch of time beyond a bend of tanning elbow,

And burning thigh, to where the poet plays
A love game with my yesterdays.
I have no zest
For exercise, no yearning after limberness

For the sake of limb alone, but enjoy,
Girlishly, this energy of Boy
That seeks to know
The meaning of *mens sana in corpore sano.*

Turning on my side, I see the shadow
Of his racket on the court grow
Long and widen
Till its very silence trespasses on the Haydn.

The Bride of Quietness

My sculptor-husband, when he was mine, possessed
Electrifying energy, humor,

The vital heat of violent force compressed
Well within a controlling frame. Few more

Creative and compelling men could fire
The clay I scarcely dared to call my soul.
Shapeless, lacking properties of higher
Existence, it was perfect for the mold

He cast me in: classic receptacle,
A thing for use but full of elegance,
An ode to Greece, forever practical,
Tellingly patterned with the hunt and dance.

My lines were lies; and yet he seemed to see
Aesthetic validation in my form.
I asked him not to draw away from me.
He said he feared he might commit some harm—

Some accidental, inadvertent hurt—
That'd shatter in an instant all the love
He'd poured out in the effort to convert
My ordinary mind to a work of

Art. And how he shuddered if I assumed
A new position or a point of view!
As if I were a royal vase entombed
After the ancient style, and the issue

Of my movement could only be a change
In where he stood, relative to his wife.
I had to perdure inanimate and strange
And still, if he would justify his life.

For I was the object of his most profound
Research, the crafty subject of his thesis,
And all I had to do to bring him down
Was let my heart break into those pieces

It ached to break into in any case.
Upon his graduation, when the guests
Had gone, and night was settling on his face,
Raising my voice above his dreams I confessed

That beauty held no truth for me, nor truth
Beauty, but I was made as much of earth
As I had been, barbaric and uncouth,
Enjoined to rhythm, shiftings, blood and birth,

And void of principle. He said he'd father
No children. I could hardly help knowing
That he'd be wrong to trust me any farther.
By sunrise it was clear he would be going

Soon. Now from time to time I see him here
And there. The shoulders have gone slack, the eyes
Conduct a lesser current and I fear
That when they catch me spying, it's no surprise

To him. He always found poetic justice
Amusing, and he knows I wait my turn.
The artist dies; but what he wrought will last
Forever, when I cradle his cold ashes in this urn.

End of Summer

I could have sworn
I saw the leaves
changing color,

the west wind torn
from the sky and bunched
into a cloud.

I could have sworn
you scorched my sleep
like lightning.

Andrei Codrescu

first blue sky

in weeks
the maintenance man
scrapes the mud-encased
leaves with a rake
the long-haired owner
of the auto hulk
pumps glue into the innards
of his life-long subject

the students get ready
to register
they are hungover
they've been courting laura

everybody's doing
whatever they can
before it rains again

often after a public event

a pretty girl curly black hair
framing literary ambition
or a shy tall boy black curly
hair burning with sympathy

will say something in a foreign
accent to me we are from bosnia
hungarians or jews my mother
was born near your city back then
it was in another country

now we are from here what should
we do with our accents

do like me I say
keep talking

a geography of poets

is all wrong, ed

what poets now live
where they say they do
where they started out
where they want to

half the midwesterners
did time in new york
the other half in california

only new yorkers write
as if they are from new york
and mostly they are not

the ones in california
were wounded elsewhere
when they feel better
or can't afford the rent
they'll go back where
they came from

this is america
you get hurt where you are born
you make poetry out of it
as far from home as you can get
you die somewhere in between

the only geography of poets
is greyhound
general motors rules them all
ubi patria ibi bene
or ibi bene ubi patria
bread out of nostalgia
not a lot of it either

some of us came from very far
maps don't help much

NICOLE COOLEY

The Red Shoes

It's always there—the world you did not believe in.

Now, without you, I will travel back
             to childhood, to the summer we moved to New Orleans,
to the yard where you are not even a shadow across the grass.

I will find August, the house beside the river,
             the blue flowers called *Impatiens* in the wood box bed,
my father's fence that keeps the men from the barges out.

I will find them again—those afternoons I hide
             in my house between the willow and the fence
where I read the fairy tales stolen from my father's drawer.

I will reenter my favorite story, become again the girl
             in mourning shoes meeting the angel whose wings reach
from his shoulders to the ground. He gives me a psalm, a broken

branch and the red shoes. Then I disobey, escape—dance
             into the center of the forest. I am free and alone.
When the angel finds me, he turns my bones to wood.

Outside the story I will live the longest summer
             of my life. Once, in my magic shoes, I will climb
the metal fence, run to the river, make my father scared.

At the edge of the river I will press my heels into the sand,
             lean forward till the men on the barges wave.
I am nine. I have never met you. I am doing the first

dangerous thing that will lead to you. Do you want to listen to my story?
             Is there a story that you want to hear? I'll tell you this—
I am giving myself away. I am beginning the walk

toward you, in my slow measured steps. I am nine.
             I am fifteen. I am twenty. I am beginning to walk toward you
without knowing you. Where are you in this long summer?

Do you ever go back to your own childhood? Do you have any story
that you want to tell? This time, the first time, my father saves me.
He calls me inside. The light falls and I turn to start for home.

I don't expect to find you on that path. Don't you see there is another world,
there are other stories before yours and mine?

Maison Blanche

My sister and I follow the long ruined avenue
to the end where the traffic winds down
like a worn-out clock, ticking the minutes

till we can count on oblivion. Here, in this old
stone building our great aunts sipped tea
as if it were gin, a parasol in every lady's glass,

wishing for ribbons and hatpins downstairs.
That was the year of gas blue dresses, jet beads,
all the husbands leaving New Orleans for the war.

Now we are looking for our other sister, the middle child
who could complete the family, the only true bride.
Between the empty floors of shoes and organza dresses

we ride the wrought iron elevator, the size of a coffin
built for two. Her grave was hand-dug and shallow
so her soul would have room to float in the open sky.

Where is she, the one who could not escape
from our mother's body? We'll look behind the glass counter,
a jar of sugar sticks wrapped in lace,

inside the pot of artificial ferns by the door,
under the chenille of the showroom's brass bed.
Is she outside, one of the angels guarding the windows?

If this were my sister's dream, she and I would find
wedding dresses in the abandoned store. Twin brides,
we spin together on the stage on the third floor

while the milliner winds baby's breath into our hair.
In that dream I am completely safe.
I want to be the heroine in someone else's story

but my own dream has nothing to do with refuge
or safety or a man gripping my shoulders.
In this other world I don't wish for a man who can save us.

Instead I want us alone, holding her small wire bones
till the rib cage lifts from her body,
the rib cage opens like an exhibit to reveal a family

of children in white dresses, all the unborn girls who know
shame and *disgrace,* now delivered.

Romance

On the train to New Orleans my sister and I
light the Virgen de Guadalupe candles
and the line of unlucky women steps out from the flame.

They file past at the window where we sit,
where we have given up being safe from them,
our four aunts with their loose dresses for mourning,

their fasting, their silent refusals. These women loved
their grief like the bread they would not let themselves eat,
like the children they would not allow into their bodies.

We know their unspoken lesson—take nothing
into the body. We know they will wait for us,
a line of dolls cut from the same sheet of butcher paper,

the sisters of this family linked by their hands and alone.
One mile into Mississippi, the train passes a statue
of blue-robed Mary in someone else's yard, bathtubs leaning

against the wire fence. I place us there. With relief,
I lower each of us into the bath, into the crystal salts.
Oil pools on the surface of the water. Sulfur is staining our skin.

The train drags on across the tracks, away from us,
leaving us in our own story. My first aunt looks down
at the flat pan of her pelvis, strung tight between hipbones

she'll never touch. She likes her body empty and clean.
Coaxing her into the tub, we preach the virtues of this water,
its power to wash away sin. The second one taps

her cigarette ash on the grass and blows smoke at the sky
while we plead with her about drowning,
tell her not to go all the way down. Why should she listen?

We know how good the body can feel, unused, expecting
nothing. But my sister and I are trying to prove them wrong.
When I kneel beside my family, I am desperate.

My sister drags the sign of the cross in the dirt
with a stick. Why don't we quit telling the story?
Once upon a time there were four princesses and a single

safe tower. No prince. In place of a man, a basket
of primroses they ripped into pieces, four finches
fighting it out for the kingdom. In another story,

my sister and I take them all home to New Orleans.
I take them all into me, my secret collection.
I give up. They live in my body. Oh, we are beautiful.

In the real story, we are all starving together. Sisters,
the wafer floats on my tongue like bad luck, like our name.

Holy Family: Audubon Zoo, New Orleans

A mother, a father, a boy child, two years old maybe.
The lovers at the end of adolescence, when the glands
call to each other, demanding such oblivion
as only another can promise for a time.
Today, free day, they have left the shelter downtown
for a park bench before the lions, the boy standing above parents
so they repeat that trinity the quattrocento did to death,
though their poverty has probably something to do with oil
and there any connection to the Holy Land begins and ends.
I will see them later, younger, older,
beneath the expressway when I drive downtown to teach,
bartering something I've never tried with an old man
who lives there any weather. Or child and mother alone
may beg the steps where the legless woman squats
at the abandoned church until police chase them away.
And the father, face expressionless as the freshmen I face later,
can disappear in the Quarter and sell himself. So may his wife.
But one of them must keep the child, their savior,
alive and well so he will have a chance.
Listen to me! Preaching! Prophesying!
Probably the boy will be traded downriver or abandoned
in a shopping center I frequent after dinner
with my wife and son. We won't turn him in,
neither of us wanting any part of this. But someone will
and he'll appear, if he's charmed, in a special
at the end of the news which I turn off, exhausted,
bored or both, if grace descends to him.

Bayou Autumn

The swans hung over the park
all summer, keeping the sun aflutter
on the lake, the naked bodies

lovers bared each other pedaling downstream
in their little boats.
                              And so I turned
inside myself, a stranger to the South,
remembering the snow of swans
molting in another weather.
I grew this skin around my own.

Now in October shadows stir
the lovers' waters. And yet the sun
washes each skin with sweat,
bristling the shore this afternoon
as ice gives way inside me,
my ribs bursting to breathe in
some other air:
                              snow, snow,
the thaw, blood thinning, spring.
And then the light steps through me
hunting for my name, I give it nothing.
I keep myself myself. I watch it go.

And watch the swans sail out
over the lake between the lovers
like clay pigeons to be shot at
by a lonely boy, this distance anywhere
darkness I've carried my whole life
& brought south, missing it till now.

Soul Making

A man takes his face into his hands,
hands which are a pool of water,
water from the faucet in the dawn-chill dark,
dark breaking up with the first birds,
birds warbling the cold pond in his palms,
palms holding him in clear reflection.

Reflection chills the man a minute:
minute, tremulous repetitions
repeating his words are falling from a tongue,
tongue bent like his knees, his hands uplifting,
uplifted. This is how a day begins,
beginning in the rhythms the water stirs,
stirring animal pools in my brain till I emerge.
This is how the I takes on the world.

Lois Cucullu

Violets

At the quarry
bottom
not scissored
by any river
but human
hand and machine
strung with cable
a clump
of violets
rides home
to wife and child
pressed
to the bottom
of a cutter's heel.

Breathing Space

My mother never told me that having sex
the first time would be like getting
water up your nose—no wonder
her book, pushed to the back of the nightstand
drawer, the one Patsy Rivette and I found
one afternoon and examined, huddled on the floor
between my parents' twin chenille-covered beds,
no wonder it said that women didn't peak
till their thirties. Whatever it meant,

that summer, Patsy and I, our bodies flat
on towels, watched the lifeguard on break
take practice dives at Audubon Park Pool,
jackknife, twist, double gainer, swan—
it looked so easy—his body splitting
the surface, the water peeling like a zipper

all the way to the bottom, then he'd flip,
slide up, nostrils streaming. He never
used the ladder.

We lay there, the sun reddening the caps
of our shoulders, the new pink flesh
the nose.

Where Things Go When They Leave

banding birds in Potomac, Maryland

Carefully unbinding the feet from the trammel
I slide the body and head through
the mesh. Its neck crooked between my fingers,

I feel its heart's muffled jab against
the meaty side of my thumb, my own pulse
a dull reply. A bird is mostly feather

and air, I remind myself, gently separating
the feathers to calculate the size of the brain,
the age, measure the wings nibbed with feathers.

The bones beneath are fragile as balsa; I check
the small amber globe of fat lodged
at the breastbone, stores for migration, note

the weight, 39 grams. The band clamped tight,
I open my hand. The thrush rights itself
and flies, swerving for a moment

like a compass needle, distancing itself
from my hand, these charts, the net hanging
slack in a sepia field.

Family Gathering
1959

The long sweat over the sink after the huge meal.
The women—aunts, mothers, grown cousins, grandmothers—
trading places in the assembly line of scrape and wash, wipe and dry.
Slow and calm. Their full cotton skirts twirling under their knees,
their hair kinked up and sprayed in place.
In some ignored corner, I undress an unconvincing plastic doll
or run my fingers over the pictures in a book and watch them
pass the dishes back and forth, the thin white cups, the vacant smiles
of expensive plates. Back and forth, they see each other in each other's
faces, materialize the reasons they've gathered again—
no holiday season, no special occasion—to stand and wash
at this double mouth of sink, to count each other and think
how old everyone else has gotten, to test the links. Now the meal is over,
the men puffing and burping on the screened side porch.
From my solitary corner, I study the men and watch
my oldest cousin Jonathan unclank his belt and lean
back sighing, and remember *Jonathan and me on a raft*
in the ocean two or three summers gone when I fell off and sunk
in gray water under gray sky of laundry suds and scum
when there was no floor no sand and I was not scared
for once looking around under the crashing waves
for once I was not scared and then there was a hand
Jonathan's hand with its gold and ruby ring
finding me in the surliness of ocean and hurting me and hurling me
up through the noisy water to the common rubber raft.
All the men are smoking and picking their teeth
with cardboard matchbook covers and flipping ashes on the floor
and spreading thighs wide on the plastic furniture, making
crinkling sounds on the slick cushions and farting and
burping and pulling smoke in and out of their slightly opened mouths.
And the women, the women moving soft in the next room with the sounds
I love, sounds like butter, and the crisp sigh the coffee can makes

when it first gets punctured. Sounds like grass, growing
when you listen close, ear on earth, deliciously silent
screams and moans you pretend you hear. The refrigerator swooshes
shut and buzzes like a heart. A high heel clicks
on linoleum. Someone is folding a sodden linen towel
and someone else is holding her hands up to the light
that falls in through the checkered curtain
and bathing them in lotion to make them soft
again. Now she is slipping on her rings and turning
up the stones to face the world.
Inside, against the fatty pad of finger flesh,
in the time- and sweat-worn silver band,
two names connected with an ampersand, and a date
twelve years from where I hover in my corner
studying the married women's placid faces and smooth hair,
remembering *the strong sounds in the bedroom that night*
I walked out of a bad dream of red water and wind
dream shaking my canopied bed like a boat   walked into theirs
and heard the sounds of animal   not family   not
Mother with the pincurls in her hair
her cold feet and furry slippers   not Father
in the suit   the late nights at work   the worn
billfold and the odor of tobacco.
The newest one is crying again and someone
must bring a breast for him to suck, someone
must smooth his head and cluck over him and wipe
his tiny penis and make him clean again.
There is noise when he sucks. There is air gasping
and infant moans deep in the throat and tiny fingers
opening and closing and the eagerness and the hunger
and the mother being sucked.
The mother rocking in the blue chair, the low lullaby
of cow and her hair a brown mirror of mine.
Now I'm thinking of the journey of the roast beef and gravy,
the coconut cake, the potato salad with little chips of pickle

and ham, all this sameness descending through bodies of kin
and turning different—blue and green and brown eyes,
four hair colors, crying babies and silent babies,
the short and the tall, the very pretty, the plum ugly.
The good going down and doing its whimsical dance and doing
different and talking in gurgles in all the stomachs
and doing its dance. Outside the other little ones
shriek and socialize and scream while they can, get dirty
while they can and touch each other everywhere while they can.
Undifferentiated bodies and voices and no urges are all urges
and the world is not a mouth it's a food.
I sit in the corner and run my fingers over the pictures
in the books and follow the symbols and signs
on the flat page and try to make them fat. Feel different
in my plaid skirt, my tortoiseshell barrette
that makes me look like all the others but funny things inside my head.
I close my eyes and feel moving, feel physics proving
right, proving it's spaces not solids, spaces and movement
inside the lines of things. Now the men are getting up and moving
inside as the sun goes under and world shudders
in a chill. The dishes are dripping in the red drainer.
The men are hitching their trousers and coughing and sucking
one last smoke. Casting their eyes around uneasily, pretending not to see
the empty places on the lawn where the tree shadows yawn
and tell them to come on anyway. In a back room, the women
are smoothing sewing patterns on a bedspread
and tickling the baby with milk on its chin and counting
the children through the bedroom window and calling them in.
And I am in my corner feeling it move under me like a body, slow and strong.
Not fast: flowing and torpid. Not weak: wide and clenching,
stretching to fit the long moment.
My hair is brown.
My father's hair is brown.
My brother's hair will soon be brown.
I see my mother's fingers in my fingers

———

47

twirling the bride doll in my lap. My fingers
busy under the covers under the ruffled canopy
what it feels like hairy down there and soft-smelling.
What it means.
My uncle's hard laugh, his glasses glinting crazily
in the first lit lamp. The scarred knees of his only son.
My glasses hooked over my ears, making everything bigger.
My grandmother's soft bun of brown hair
going gray. And the baby holding the deep hem
of her dress and pulling like I did,
at one, over the furnace's heated grid, falling
and burning crisscross nests of pinkish scars
on my lower legs. Now I cover them up. Now
I trace them with my finger. Now my father
still doesn't know how to touch me. He sees my scars
and puts his hand like a crown on top of my head
too roughly and it hurts. Then it's gone.
He's gone and the unintended roughness starts
soaking into the strange universe of movement around me,
into the dance that danced me so impossibly here
from these strangers' tall and barricaded bodies
to my own small collection of flesh and bone.

ALBERT BELISLE DAVIS

What They Wrote on the Bathhouse Walls
Yen's Marina, Chinese Bayou, LA

I

February leafing
willowed through
our window nets

In the tent
we wondered
if the world was winter-gone

II

I am too long
longing among
the strangers

I am
a foreign girl
am Bombay girl

Uptown 2–4540

III

The kiss is better
when I shut her up
when I startle back the last word
and it falls prisoned
lashed behind her eyes

IV

If I could set my table
before he leaves
a goblet of claret
a rhino horn fork and a plate
I would eat his thin form
send him sliding
down my gullet
warm with brickred wine
the flour of his flesh

V

I am feast
for your nose
parsley scent in sweat
cardamom in sari
no regret

Uptown 2–4540

VI

Tell my lawyer to tell the lawyer
of my wife to tell my wife
I will remember us
that day before the fall
at noon
that day we stood
in an aspen hollow
steps before the wood
Our lungs hurt from
the short hike from
the truck
We sought
nothing more than breath

Tell him to tell him
to tell her
I will forget all
that would follow
after noon
I will remember us
before the fall
september early on us
the yellow light of aspen on us
seconds before we caught
our breath
in the quiet hollow
short steps before the wood

VII

Fast please
under this matchless moon
come let us
kindle sloe-eyed night

Uptown 2–4540

Culs-de-sac

She wakes up cold from her nap.
Outside the rain has stopped.
The bridge is still closed for repair
the traffic at detour. In the orchard
the rooster still pecks at himself in the mud.
The roof of the empty fruit vendor's stand
reflects sunset at roadside
the citrus spectrum, the yellows, red.
She does not leave her bed.

She thinks of New England
four weekends a year in the family cabin
woodlands making sense of season
a color shift for each divide.
No divides exist along the bayou. In a year
through her window she has seen
two wet seasons meet in continuous green.
The whole overlaps the whole.
Land and water meld to marsh,
sky and earth to horizon.
Without care, thought becomes that suspension
of mind and brain
she peers into on days of rain.

Her mother taught her to cook.
Her father sold locks for his pay.
She left them in Westport at thirty-three
but brought with her her knack
for eating in, for latching dark metaphor out.
Her lover left her for less
for an Indian with braces and palmetto egress.
She has been alone for three days now.
Well-fed, with her window bolt set
what has she to fear in loneliness
the solitary black pecking bird?
She will wake herself early, burn flour for roux
devour with sunrise some hot chicken stew.

She listens once for rain
then sleeps again and dreams
of nectarines and wakes and screams
as she bundles her sheets on her lap.

Proposing to A Victoria

Today they call her A Victoria
not because of a house of five
she alone survived a strain of virus
Great War breezes carried to her sisters
but because the strain of facing her
infected the hope of the hardiest men in town.
Kneeling under her smile one caught cold;
in the moss shed he offered garnet and sneezes.
One, an embezzler, found himself so bold
as to face her in the soundless absolute
of a banker's office on a federal holiday.
Like all men before, before he asked
he tried to tantalize with things that shine:
a silver nugget on a silver chain.
Her *no*, his moan, a cracking chair splat
echoed off the skylight and the friezes.
He revived himself enough to say,
rising to the limits of his suit
and pointing to his silver on her chest,
"You have a piece of metal for a heart."

She kept his bauble and his gift of truth
for truth delivered coldly is a prize.
She was not another heartless beauty
living on the bayou's edge in town.
She buried those whose beauty she replaced
and wears a piece of metal on her heart.
Of all their gifts she kept only that.

Once she also gave a gift of truth.
The night he made his call, she had begun
the common-law liturgy of the single bed, had hung
her necklace on the corner of her mirror.
She does not recollect their faces, but remembers
this one shivered holding out an orange
under the moon the second night of a *coup de nord.*

"Wind's in the bayou flue," she said. "Be quick."
He did not speak. "I know why you're here," she said
taking the orange. "Ask."
                    "My brother . . ."
                                        "Quick."
"He saw you on your porch before the war.
He also saw you after his return.
I've come because of him. He asked me to ask."
She had heard such words before, from others
who stood in stead before her. She'd sent them away.
As she started to do the same with this one, he said,
"My brother died fifteen years ago."
She knew what the dead could make of a living sister,
knew that one could dream of the dead, could long
even live with the dead instead of marry.
But what was to be made of one live brother?
She felt for the lump of metal beneath her shawl
remembered it on the quicksilver edge of her vanity.
Bringing the orange in stead under her shawl
she said, "Be quick or the wind will have us all."

"His first day back in town, on our way to the bank
we stopped in front of your house. My brother told me
about the beautiful sisters he had seen.
Instead of five, we saw one, in green.
Behind my brother, one foot off the banquette
I watched as he called and asked you your name.
You turned away. In town they gave us your name
and told us of four headstones you'd left blank.
They also told us oranges wouldn't grow
in the cheap clay between the cypress swamp
and the fertile Chinese Bayou levee.
Our signatures alone began the account
that got us the house where Chinese Bayou turns
the first time it denies it's headed south.

Two weeks after we'd seen you on your porch
my brother told me, coughing in the rays
of the kerosene lamp that had started our second account,
'You must ask for Victoria's hand, not I.
Marriage is like the grafting we must do.
She and I are both the same trunk stock.'

"I started to say I would not have the courage.
Instead I asked about his cough and why
he'd stayed away for five years after the war.
He said, 'A fog as green as Victoria's dress
made lace of my lungs. Three years I cursed God, gambled
until my losing and his silence were proof
he did exist. Then I cursed him and gambled two more.'

"My brother told me you could wait till spring.
In spring there'd be another loan to get
and we'd drive together into town.
By then we'd have worked at what would be ours to have.
Oranges. A family. Good names.
Collateral with branches through the years.
We had the winter to talk, much clay to wet.

"My brother went for the loan before the spring
in January of the record freeze.
He returned in February for another.
Each time he pulled dead sticks from the holes
he replaced them all with dormant trunk and twig.
Each time he returned from the frozen field, he said,
'We will have, my brother, what's ours to have.'
That year the second February freeze,
which one mile farther south on the brackish shore
peeled the plywood hulls off pirogues, took
all the orange trees and the rest of my brother.
The night he died, my brother had no cough.
Under blankets bankers owned, he shook.

When he asked, 'Our name? Victoria?'
I told him that I'd see you before the frost
had melted off the bark and grafting scars.
I waited till dusk to bury him with my lie
in the cypress an arpent behind the house.
Then I burned his unpacked duffel bag
and watched a red glow die in the black of the trees."

She said, "And you have come to rectify
after fifteen years."
                              "Yes."
                                      "Why?"
He said, "I've been dreaming of my brother,
waking from the same dream every morning.
He owned no suits. But I see him in a brown suit.
We have left a room, ours, but there's a desk.
We are standing in front of a kitchen table, ours,
when he falls. I hold him. He is old.
His skin is white, shallow, like frost over clay
and his eyes are small, yellow and hard, like the marbles
in the Chinese Checker game we used to play.
I say to him, 'You are alive again.
That is all that matters. Stop.'"
                                      "And why,"
she asked, "are you still here? You've done
enough of what you've come to do."
                                      "No," he said,
"I want what my brother wanted for us. Please . . ."

She does not recollect their faces, but remembers
lies that would not die in the black of the trees.
That night, she looked to the gate where grocers left
the food and fled in the influenza days
and bringing the cold zest out from shawl, she said,
"I know what your brother knows only in dreams. In death
and in life, you will not have what you shall not have."

Not a Bad Place to Start

Bodies tucked away
like packets of honey:
the folds of the morgue
are sweet with the death
   of winos. Those
who've survived
another December night
read signs in the clouds
of their stinking breaths
and warm their fingers
at the fire barrel.
These guys the salt of
will inherit the earth
(but maybe not this morning).
Among Jake's stories
the one of Elijah
grizzled houseguest
covering the young boy's body
with the pall of his own:
chemistry of conversion,
death to life! Jesus too
cried 'rise!' and his friend
like a kite in a sudden wind
rose. Still good news?
Someone's shaking Willie
but he won't wake up.
Only groans: having reached
this advanced stage of life
he has let it be known
he won't get up
for any old reason
for just anyone at all.
First he must know
who's calling and what

they have to offer.
Hard bargain, picky Willie
but not such a bad place
    to start.

Birdsong: Analogues

> As a new poem is made . . . past voices are
> convoked—to be changed, little or much, by the
> addition of another voice.
>
> —Wendell Berry

      *

What can one bird add to flight, to song?
Dark tanks whine and rumble across desert sand,
muzzles quiet for the moment but hot and black
with firing; what can one prisoner (Lt. Col. John B.,
mother's son, husband, high-school hero for his game
saving free throw against rival crosstown Bulldogs)
beaten to cringing and paraded before enemy cameras
for his "to be or not to be" soliloquy, tell us about
war? Do those in heaven hear an unbroken chorus,
the dark strains an undergirding, streaks of blood
like a cello's moan marbling the "pip-pipping"
of a female cardinal, dull colored in backyard oak,
    fluffing against the dripping cold?

      *

Somewhere the sparrow falling.
Somewhere arrowing praise. Somewhere a possum
ground like hamburger into the steamy blacktop.
Through open window a piano is pouring into rain,
a young boy works at B. B.'s wail: thrill, thrill,
gone, gone! A seed is sprouting in a dead stump
somewhere, somewhere the weather means business:
banana leaves cold-blackened in a night, melted like wax,

fat jays wallow in the feeder, heron stalks
a polluted ditch: splendor in squalor. Somewhere
a rapist sizes then seizes his prey. A prayer
like incense lifts. Insects sift among the dead
leaves like monks. A soprano coats her throat
with olive oil and sings into the stirring pot. What
    will she add to this ancient song?

*

And what can this jogger possibly add
to prayer? She slows then stops at golf course
fourth hole pond to watch for a moment dabs of mist
corkscrew off its mirrored surface, disappear into
a swelling sun. Arms at her side, she is mystified
by an antique voice that also rises, saying:
"It is meet to praise, Jill; meet and right so to do!"
As great-grandmother's mustiness blossoms in the dawn,
she recollects, smiles, repeats, adding something
    of her own and running on.

The Inheritance of Death in the Vesture of Dance

The Kwakiutl tribe of the Northwest Coast
has been studied beyond its death. Even now,
as we read this poem together, the ghost

of a shaman is showing a scholar how
the "hamatsa" dance was done. Frame by frame
the dance unfurls, the long-dead dancer sows

the meaning of the bird-monster whose name
was Kwakwakwanooksiwae or
"Raven-at-the-mouth-of-river." The same

savage long-beaked spirit which lured
boys across that river and its terror
into manhood now hops and twists, captured

in an island of light. The projector's whir
forces the flickering, washed-out image
into the dark, all but empty room where

the scholar jots it into footnote, page
until, tired, he runs it backward on its reel.
Weren't you beckoned to becoming at some age

by steps such as these? I watched my father steal
a storm from Chesapeake, throwing our ketch
against howl until we rocked, unreal,

and I pitched and washed in the fear of death.
And he let me, unmoved by my fear or his own
until the storm had spent on us its meanest breath.

He'd danced into my life the dance of stone.
In Pointe Coupee I saw a father give a son
a single movement. We stood in pasture grown

in ryegrass, this man and I. While his son
played, we talked business. Midsentence he stopped,
reached into his pickup, unpacked his gun,

a .22, stepped four paces, shouldered, popped
one shot into some brambles—a rattler
five feet long. The boy sang out, leaped and hopped

delight, sudden heir to a gesture
that plucked from the instant with quickness, skill,
the flower of death, death in the vesture

of dance. The big snake's grave made a small hill.
As father had no doubt learned, so had he taught.
When it came to the boy, he'd know how to kill.

The scholar makes his way to the parking lot
through the sleeping campus. The shaman
should be sleeping, too, buried in his plot

of history or, as they say, "in the can."
But he's not. Drums rumble. The dark quivers
with the movement of wings. The scholar's a man

moved for a time beyond words, those slivers,
moved for a moment to take up with chance,
to stop in the terror of that constant river,

moved for a moment to dip in and dance.

John Doucet

Le Charivari de Celestin Joseph Doucet

Plattenville, 10 August 1867

Through wetting, emerald eyes her mind burns
Flush its opaline face. I take her head,
Hardened plow-hands comb her hair's soft turns,
And lay my sacred dreams onto our bed.

I breathe the humid fall of August night
Rising from her skin. My eyes fold closed to still
Her image eclipsing the candlelight.
The silent field beyond the curtained sill

Is stirred by a cackling spirit raised to life:
*Celestin-Joseph! C'est l'esprit jaloux
De ta Rosalie Cat'rine!*—my first wife
In the villagers' shrill voices made true.

They drummed iron pots and pans and sang my name
Across the pastures. Torches marked their shadows
Through my brightened room. I stood in shame,
A naked figure framed in veiled windows.

A swift August chill protecting her grace,
Retreating beneath her whitening trousseau,
My new bride implores through a cooling face,
Va faire du café et des petites gateaux.

Freshman with a Neuroanatomy Text

Mind, but flesh. Out from the glossy text,
The mind is made real yet stray, yet perplexed.
Stains and drawings are witless to find
The electric paths of thought defined
By the timeless caution of evolution.

At once, both problem and pure solution,
One billion fibers synapsed in tandem,
The flesh of logic is cruelly random.

Le Feu-Follet

In the earth's gravid bed
A small unchristened head
In laced white linen dressed
Calm, unsimpering rests.

Fleshless ire vapors free,
Low floats over night sea,
With silent vexing finds
Sleepless fishermen's minds.

Earthly play ended fast.
A vigorous spirit lasts
And unlanguishing vents
In pure malevolence.

CLARISSE DUGAS

Children and a Great Aunt

We called her Tante Amenthe.
We never knew who he was
or why she married him
and by the time I knew her
she had lost her hair,
wore a red wig, always askew
as though she had no time
for such things.
He died, leaving her a farm
with animals in the middle of town.
She took care of them
wearing muddy oversized boots,
carrying a stick to prod them along.
There was a parrot in the dining room
whose one line was, "Where's Joe?"
She had no children.
In her coffin, she wore the red wig
and we wondered if the boots
were in there too.

Eulogy for the Sears-Roebuck Catalog
1993

The year FDR died
we lived on small allotments
in my father's town:
house borrowed from an uncle—
half of it closed off,
car parked in a musty garage,
food measured out in stamps
from a book lost while I
skipped to the corner grocery.

My mother, inconsolable,
forgot to roll her hair
worn round like a sausage,
took to her bed
and pulled the covers up.
"See what you did?" my father
rasped, shaving blocked ice,
splinters stinging my arms and face
as I stood close,
already tasting sherbet.

The invalid recovered,
wore a green chenille robe, ordered
Christmas gifts from Sears-Roebuck.
I prowled through closets,
poked in chiffonier drawers,
found, finally, the bracelet
with gold-like hearts
hidden there for me.

Later, we moved to my mother's town:
lived in her inherited house,
ate Borden's ice cream
from cups with tiny wooden spoons,
wore voile and dotted swiss dresses,
walked to the graveyard and cleaned
family tombs, placing flowers under markers
with names like Ursule, Solange, Clarisse.

Sac-à-lait

She sits and eats *courtbouillon*,
savors bits of fish as they slide
down her throat, thinks of Henry James
whose people are too refined for meals.

Baked snapper had been intended.
The party had left at dawn last week,
driven forty miles, then more
by boat in the gulf to find them.
Rods with several hooks had allowed
for pulling in three or four at a time.
Bruises in her armpits still remind
of resented fragility.

But today, perch seemed easier to fix,
ladled on rice when done.
As a door slams suddenly,
she swallows, startled.
A bone lodges.
She drinks water,
eats bread,
finally calls a doctor who
says to come to his office.

On the way, she thinks of
the Monet print not yet found,
the scent of ginger lilies,
garbage to be put out on Tuesday.

Spine against the wall now,
she holds her breath.
The curved tool
probes its way down,
finds its catch.

CHRISTINE DUMAINE

Bathing Father

I cover my hand
with a wash cloth,
turn over and over
the bar of soap,
coating your body
with a film, thin
as dragonfly wings.
Your eyes close.
I keep swathing
you in milk.
When I touch your arm,
it lifts.

And here on the back
of your hand the veins
turn a bluer lapis not
in the bath.
It is the same
hand that held mine
when we visited
Mammoth Cave
in the fifties.
We walked among
the spots of light hung
from makeshift wires.
There was the constant
mineral drip, the pitch
black where nests of bats
hid, their rodent
claws needled in clay.

The reward was a mile
from the cave mouth.
In the hypnotic darkness,
tourists lined the rim

of a shallow pool.
Even then my hand
had begun to slip
out of yours as our
faces took on the oil
gloss of the cave walls.
The guide clicked
his flashlight.
And there, in the luminous
circle, blind fish
battled for a place
in the painful glare.
White and supple,
they were thin
as the fallen
camellia petals
that scattered our lawn
each spring.

     Lately,
I feel the features
of my face, touch who
you once were, the blunt
nose, the shape of bone
around my eyes.
You are young in me.
And as I silken the breasts
that have come to you
late in life, that hang
empty as purses, I notice
the small pale creature
hovering under your belly
so swollen with age,
its fragile waiting,
a plea to enter the body
that made it.

You know the routine.
I turn the hot and cold
spigots, and you seem to awake.
Today, you sigh deeply.
As a swirl of shampoo
fills the center of my palm,
as it has for the last two years,
you bow slowly toward
the steaming drizzle of light.

River Witch

I sent you to the barges
when time was crawling
on slow baby knees.
The children need bread.
She saw you and envied
the pure breath of our love
flowing like light through your veins.
Every day she watched you,
her long head bending & swaying
at the weight of men and barges.
She courted you with her mud songs.
Your thoughts belonged to me,
             washed nightly
in the olive oil of our love.

When you were there
the steel and wood of the barge floor
protected you from her potions.
In the cold river night
she played the mandolin for you
             called your name,
but my love wrapped itself
around you like a blanket.

That day she coiled her long wet body
around the barge
whispered for you to come,
when you didn't answer
she heaved & tossed her slimy head up
pulled at your legs;
heaving, swishing, & turning,
she tilted the barge.
When the men tried to save you
she held them back

with her nine hundred and ninety-nine hands,
plucked you in with the thousandth one.
You fought her
but she fought with mind,
rocks, boat parts, and time.
She churned herself like butter
sucked your spirit out.
            You were gone,
gone like yesterday is gone.

            I go to her
with oils, fruits, and flowers
begging her to give you up,
birth you from whatever
fish belly you are in
but she ignores me.

Nightly I call for you
on the river bank;
with naked feet I run
calling your name
with a net for your soul
if it should pass me in the wind.
One day I will fish you from her
            take you home
like a captured sacalait.

Practicing

I hear grandma breathing
            loud and rasping.

The doctor says she is sleeping,
but I know she is practicing,
learning to be dead.

The body is teaching itself to be still,
to do nothing for ages and ages.
To stop reaching out to open a door.
Unlearn "Ha ya do?" and "Want some coffee?"

Forget how to bring the cup up
from table to lip
                    to sip,
forget how to sip.

Lose the path to the garden,
discontinue dressing and undressing.
All the things that took all childhood
                    to memorize.

She opens her eyes sometimes
without recognition
                    without seeing;
already she has forgotten how to see.

The eyelids, awkward rusty hinges
holding two doors to nowhere:
nothing comes in, nothing goes out.

Her spirit is walking,
                    a cat in a forest
                    a child following a bird.
It has nowhere to go, no direction.

It is learning to misplace paths.
It must have no place to go, no purpose,
                    rambling in endless sleep.

The doctors say soon,
but she has already lost time.
She can no longer read a clock face
or follow the sun across the sky
                    in and out of day.

"Soon" means nothing to her.
She is remembering an open space,
choosing to enter or not enter.

She goes forward,
changes her mind,
sits waiting
for Gyp the dog or Corsey the cow,
calls for Ben, the long-dead husband.

She has left with all those dead things.
Her body doesn't know;
it hasn't discovered its death.

First Gift

God made this world
like a crystal ball.
Robed it in colors:
flowers of red,
mountains of brown,
valleys of green,
          seas of blue.
He carved this world,
holding it carefully in his hands.
Dug out gullies, built up mountains,
ribboned with rivers,
peopled with fish.
Hollowed out caves
for dwellings of beasts.
Planted gardens
for pleasures of men.
          Named it "earth."
Gave it to Adam
who shared it with Eve

then passed it to Seth and Cain
who sent it to Noah,
to Abraham, to Isaac & Jacob.
Jacob willed it to his kin,
who left it to my kin,
who passed it to my grandparents,
who tied it in sugar cane leaves,
        gave it to my parents.
They held it in their eyes,
and planted it with mustard greens,
decorated with marigold,
rooster combs and zinnias.
When I was old enough
they took me outside.
        My father pointed up
        to show me the sky.
Touching wood and greenness
        he said: "tree."
God made this world and gave it to me.
        Mother scooped up a handful of dirt.
She picked up an acorn:
dirt, earth, seed, world.
        Say "world."
My father plucked a pear from the tree,
        bit into it,
gave me a piece.
The rain fell,
he opened his mouth.
I opened, tasted, touched, smelled.
God gave this to us,
we give it to you.
Receive this earth,
nourish and tend it,
feed it and feed from it.
Hold, love, and keep it.

And when the time comes
give this world,
precious, improved,
      to your son.

JOHN FINLAY

The Bog Sacrifice

The iron and acid water of the bog,
Rising and falling with the winter rains,
Two thousand years, preserved him as he died,
Pinned naked to the floor by wooden crooks.
No fire had cut and cleaned the clotted soul.
Runic stakes, washed white as salt, were laid
Over his narrow breast, sunk in the peat.

The sacrificial rope they hanged him from,
Of woven skins, still cut into his throat,
Tight as when death came. His gentle face,
Forced upward by the torsion of the noose,
Bore with monstrous discipline his bane,
As loose ends, like serpents, meandered down
His naked length, pressed into his flesh.

A cap of wolfskin hived his shaven head.
Descended from a line of conscript priests,
He died in youth, still delicate and whole.
When he was lifted from the pit, the earth
Itself then sweating like an ancient beast,
He looked as if alive. Faint cries of snipes
Brought sunlight piercing to his closing eyes.

Before Christ reached this isolated north,
A chthonic goddess, holding iron breasts,
Each year in early spring exacted death.
In winter when the winds blew keen off ice,
Or summer with its rippling swarm of weeds,
The bog seemed never raised above the sea,
But underneath, out of whose depths she came.

Audubon at Oakley

My Gallic cunning poured sweet wine into
The calyxes of trumpet-vines and caught
Small drunken birds a bullet blows apart.
Others I shot, pinned them to a board
To draw the fresh-killed life. Elusively,
This *is* that quickens in the living eye
Escaped the sweat of art, and drying ink.
I tore blind pages till I reached the one
That pleased my avid mind. The wilderness
There teems with birds I never saw before:
White and wood ibises, the sparrow hawk,
The red-cock woodpecker, and painted finch.
I hunted them for days and nights until
I throve in timelessness. One day stood out.
The fall was blazing in the silent trees;
Wedges of geese were passing overhead.
I heard below all things the river sough.
I saw my book, taut wings of mockingbirds
In combat with the snake knotted beneath
The nest, its open mouth close to the eggs,
Now held forever in the lean, hard line.
And underneath, defining them, combined:
The clean abstraction of their Latin names,
The vulgate richness of this Saxon salt.

Note: Oakley is a plantation home outside St. Francisville, Louisiana, where Audubon
lived and worked during the summer and fall of 1821.

Thinking About Taniece
Buried in St. Augustine Churchyard, 1968

You will recognize my people
from Lafayette, Crowley,
from Opelousas, Abbeville,
from Eunice, Basile, and Mamou,
by the way the forehead slopes gently,
by the rounded noses,
and by the syllables
that stumble out, staccato
in English.
Once I was ashamed
to be a Cajun.
The city people said
we were ignorant,
and we believed them.

But now I love my grandfather,
pauvre défunt Taniece.
He was handsome and American.
He looked like Lincoln,
mole on his cheek and all.
He said *shit* in French
half a dozen times a day.

And one Easter,
deep in the woods,
he lifted the heavy lid
of his iron pot,
peeked in,
doffed his cap with a bow,
and said in French:
Hello, Rabbit,
Fontenot's my name!

N'Oncle Oréneus

If you saw my great-great uncle
who died when I was barely 12,
he would not tell you
how the wagon came rolling fast at him,
how he tripped and fell, how the left back leg
of his favorite horse touched his spine
as a doctor would touch it, and how the wheels
of the wagon gently separated his shoulder.
He looked different. His shirts looked as if
they hid a large watermelon on his back
where the wagon and his favorite horse
once betrayed him. No, he was more like
Atlas carrying the world on his back,
under his shirt. I was barely 12 and thought:
someone let the air out of his back! Or he will
rise forever among clouds, among tall trees.
He kissed my forehead. He gave me his best fiddle.
In French he asked me:
"You think they'll find a coffin to fit me?"
pointing to his giant world, laughing.

The Derrick Man

At midnight, in water deeper than sky,
The derrick man climbs the drilling rig
Rung by slippery rung to his willowy platform
Ninety feet above floor, above roughnecks, above lights.

The clamor of diesel engines softens gradually
To a muffled groan. He straps himself loosely
Inside the leather harness and leans out
Across the tangle of men and machines far below,

A trapeze artist with no net, suspended
In his leap. Stout sleeveless arms reach outward
And embrace each new stand of steel pipe,
Pulling it into position for the hardhats below.

The Gulf air presses with vaporous gravity
And his black curls dampen with mist and sweat.
He flexes half-laced boots to loosen his ankles,
A trick skier leaning for the jump.

Repetition cushions the danger and the moist hours
Stretch out like patches of fog ascending.
Then just south of the rig lights he sees them
Buoy upward in dance. One by one

Silvery porpoises lift silently from dark water,
Remain suspended for a moment
And, sudden as a single feather, disappear.
Later they emerge in pairs perfectly synchronized

Performing for him. Two, then four, then eight,
All in rhythm. He dreams of being home, gliding low
Around deep curves on his cycle, speeding alone at dawn
On a back-bayou highway, pearl black and smooth.

A north breeze heavy with salt air moves him
To turn his head skyward. A trillion colored stars

Stare back into the map of his eyes.
Far from everything, from everyone, in orbit.

No stop signs, no trees, no streetlights. No ceiling.

Sky Music

The first cold front has passed over our town
And cleansed our air. I open the windows
To let George Winston's piano reverberate

Off the topaz and ruby trees. The wind that splays
The branches is so brazen I can't concentrate.
Even birds don't fly on a day like today;

They know that let loose in all this blue,
Like balloons from a child's hand,
They would never return to earth.

Over a hundred miles out in the Gulf
The water blazes with such iridescence
That when the excursion boat ties up to the rig,

The fishermen can only lay down their poles
And stare into the blue, knowing the fish
Are deeper down than stars, impossibly far.

I look in the mirror to wash my cold face:
A six-year-old at her First Communion,
The face lit up with longing, eyes startled blue

As the new glass rosary rinsed over her pressed
Hands, a mouth set wide at the net white veil.
Only the beauty spot under her left eye remains

Unchanged. Doors keep opening and I am porous
As piano music. The sky reaches inside and pulls
Everything upward. The roof grumbles, ashamed.

Stepping outside I am disoriented, happy, removed
As a paper doll from its page of sky. All I want
Is to sit under crayon-colored trees, share

A thermos of café angelica with a man I met last week,
And untie the soaked rope that holds the loaded barge
Of my future. I wish it would all float away—

This whole house, heaped with bookcases,
Albums, sofas, plans to publish and marry—
Leaving nothing but me, the ruby trees,
And the music swandiving off the leaves.

Offshore Fog: Day Twelve

Homicidal fog has us trapped here
one more delirious day, sick of each other
and this platform wrapped in seaweed stickiness
and the urine-smelling Gulf of Mexico.

I refuse meals and talk, hoping to induce coma.
No boats to save us, the chopper grounded,
murky mists still rolling in from salty forever:
this is the fog that penetrates even the sane.

With a nod, the welder's mask drops
in front of his face. I look away.
The searing rod sizzles slowly into steel,
sparks fly like neon sawdust, mesmeric.

Visible only in patches, the water glares
with the silver pink of mercury spilled.
He lifts up, I grind the bubbly seam
to a perfect bracelet. He bends

to the next pass, the seductive dance
of the blinding arc snatches at my eyes.

Look away, a saving voice floats up
from the bottom, *forget him, look away.*

Below, a jellyfish slinks and sleethers
unabashed. The floppy brim of its body
is a lacy summer hat tossed off a wharf
in despondence, the three bright yellow roses

soaked and faded to diaphanous beige. The woman
presses her face into her hands and weeps.
There is nothing left but the wharf
and the sun and the too extravagant hat

floating slowly to sea. And the woman
rests her head back, squints into a fire-
laced moon, colder corona than eye can adore,
but doesn't feel its burning . . .

so I shout *look away* with a voice that floats up
from the bottom, *forget him, look away.*

NORMAN GERMAN

New World in the Morning

Somewhere on the outskirts
of a southeast Texas town
where you burn your neighbor's house
for revenge
and then your own for insurance money
to leave the country,
the Zen Buddhist basketball team
is practicing for its next game.

Friday night on the court,
at peace with themselves,
the fans, the refs, and other players,
they make their baskets every time
and never trip their opponents on fast breaks
or pull their shorts down on jump shots.

Flowing to the rival end of the court
they politely step aside as the Cobras'
star player drives for a lay-up and,
having nothing to fight for, misses.

Waiting underneath, docile as a doe,
Sardria Char opens his hands
like a baby bird's mouth, open in praise.

Avoiding the karma-disturbing thuds of a dribble,
he takes the ball and hands off to Krishna
who passes to Gandhi sitting cross-legged,
sleepy-eyed under the hometown hoop.
Without looking, Gandhi flings the ball skyward.
The ball rises in a perfect silent curve.
Never touching the rim, it swishes through the net
like a good soul coming into being.

Tonight they subdue with serenity.
Next year they take the title.

Whitey Goes Long

Dusk bore down on us at six,
blurring our white thermals stiff with frost
dotting the east side of the Collins field.
On the west a line of leafless trees
etched their names on a corpse-gray sky:
chinaberry, tallow, mimosa, tallow, tallow, fig.
And the elm that last year intercepted T-Boy
for fifteen stitches.
The skins had the south goal, a two-lane blacktop.

It was the last play of our last day as children.

"This is it, wimps," Lambchop said, fingering patterns
on his palm. "Tripper, you and Five Nickels
take down Heavy, clip him if you have to. Crane,
spumoni special, then buttonhook and sit.
Bobbles and Rooster, cross in the middle
to jam up the zone. Whitey, you'll be wide open.
We're staking our lives on you. Go long."
He traced the route off his hand.
"I mean *long*. In the road if you have to."

"Thirteen! Sixty-four! Huppity-HUT! HUT!"
Lambchop faded back, Heavy went down, the sky
brightened as the sun dropped below a cloud.
The ball whipped from his hand, wobbled a moment,
and straightened out. At the edge of the field,
Whitey looked back, up, then out beyond the street
where he would meet the ball
that sailed above the highest highline
with no thought of coming down.
He jumped the ditch like a deer.
Two cars scissored as he crossed the yellow stripe
and came out in the clear, opening his stride.
"Long!" we hollered as the ball shrank to a dot.

Both teams ran to the ditch where even the shirts,
hands cupped to their mouths, screamed,
"Long, Whitey! You gotta go *long*!"

Somewhere, in fluid concentration,
he is still running.
Someday, fifty or so years up the road,
the ball will spiral down into sixth grade.
To be there, I'd give away my best year:
to hear the speed of the spinning ball
kiss to a stop in his outstretched hands.

The Space Between Stars

There are pictures of pinwheel galaxies
meeting at right angles,
cutting into each other like buzz saws.
And yet, the astronomers say,
no two stars will collide.

I believe this only because yesterday
I saw the woman I was cut away from
at the beginning of time,
my perfect opposite.

When our eyes met, we knew.
I pushed my chair back,
as she did hers,
and we started for one another.
At the moment of impact—
not one molecule, not one atom of mine
touching one of hers—
our bodies passed
right through each other.

John Gery

What It's Like to Travel Long Distance Alone on the Train

There's the sitting, quietly. And something else—
the long, vague expectation of a rising
like a great white heron from some green marsh cove
another fifty miles or so down track
to get a drink of water. There're the lights
from unfamiliar spots you recognize,
those landmarks two more blocks or two more towns
from where you start anticipating them.
And passengers, the restless ones, wend by
imagining by walking backwards they,
in quantum leaps, will outwit time. They glance
at you, as you in glancing out the window
imagine who it is they think you are,
how little or how much they make of your
impassive stare, the title of the book
it seems you've just looked up from, as though words
when read on trains take longer to digress from,
or the distance from your point of origin
(some indeterminate shore in the past)
to where you're headed, near to, but beyond,
the place you really mean to go. There's sleep,
a public sleep you dip into and out of
with gull-like ease, in skittering ascent,
until your slackened body's not enough
to hold your private thoughts, and with it dreams
of perfect stillness, propped upright, the calm
of evenings when deep in an easy chair
your every nerve accepts the air. You will
each moment, smell each mile. You count each stop,
how many stops there'll be before your stop:
Eight, seven, six, five, four . . . There's not much more,
except, of course, the landscapes, cities, dumps,
damp stations filled with waving families

and friends, unknown to you but intimate,
their every tear, once you regain full speed
in your uncertain journey toward the sun,
infecting your slow thought with sudden care
for what you know you'll never have again.
And as you turn from them and watch the sky,
you whisper to yourself, *good-bye! good-bye!*

No Elegy for One Who Died Too Soon

Some things escape us: useful days, free hours,
earned dollars, hate we shouldn't have stopped holding,
heat we hope will break in afternoon showers,
a shower inconveniently unfolding

itself like a curtain let down from a rafter
on a giant stage that frames the street we pass
en route from work to home, from now to after,
the in-betweens, the images in glass

that two or three of us made once while strolling
downtown in that small city, outflung ropes,
the smiles in photographs, the awkward calling
hundreds of miles across high wires, hopes

that snap, hopes that don't, stealing a nap
or listing in a boat—these get away
from us. But we're to blame for what has hap-
pened here. And we're to blame each time we say,

"Things get away," without then understanding
the ones who understand but don't know how,
the ones who sleep late, who have trouble landing
a job that pays, who wear their hats too low

pretending confidence, who brave a storm
to feel its penetrating blow, who sail
alone to kill the pain that keeps them warm.
Things get away. He won't come back.

To a Friend's Wife

There is a pain so delicate
we consider it luxurious
to suffer—walking into
a spiderweb across an eyelid
or catching the tiny chaff
of broken bits of eggshell
in the throat. To you,
dear friend, I owe this pain.

Such a pleasure it is to sit
with you by my shoulder
when mildly I can tell,
though your clear gaze is hid
as we page through your photographs
and in my voice I feign
a calm, that we are a spurious
pair, who can say nothing bolder
than we are not alone,
we are not alone.

QUO VADIS GEX-BREAUX

Jazz Rain

She had a kind of classy coarseness
like raw silk
a kind of open earthiness
without being dirt
a way of saying things
that made them seem something
more than she meant
(sometimes a little less)

She moved with the breezes
without being flighty
capturing men's hearts
before they realized surrender
also meant their minds

She grew up with water sounds
split splat splat
on tin roofs
soft tappings on bare windowpanes
tip tip tip
after heavy cloudbursts

Rooms where she had been
danced alone and empty for hours
after she left
replaying her laughter
that fell like jazz rain
a slow, smooth, syncopated harmony
bursting later in thunderous
improvisational splendor
intricately weaving patterns
from rainbowed puddles in her head

Choice few could hear her music
read the notes to which she danced
hers was too cloistered an intellect

to teach steps meant only for the select
who knew how to scat between life's drops
plish, plish, plish
do wa-a-a-a-a-a-a

Solo she sang her own harmonies
overdubbed and lightning sparkled
simply percussioned, softly strung
with wind-whistling horns
she glistened, spontaneous, evolving
defined by blues bridges
a wet, unfinished song.

The Long and Short of It

To every jazz aficionado
or would-be
who has wondered
what Professor Longhair was doing
with his left hand and how
know that it was gumbo and crawfish étouffée
screened-in porch sitting on hot summer nights
fighting the anyway mosquitoes
while waiting for that welcome breeze
from the river, bayou, or lake

Know that it was Carnival, the season
with balls and trashy throws
at day / night parades
and Mardi Gras, the day
with Indian songs and Zulus and
you too, you Mardi Gras

For all who wondered about what makes
New Orleans food so smack-yo-lips good
and music so snap-yo-fingers rhythmic

know that our ancestors always could
make much of little and taught us how
to add a beat here, a spice there
to change that thing
you once recognized
into something you're aching
to get to know.

Plantation

Now, at dusk, beyond the river's slow strokes
and the migraine of mosquitoes, I almost see
her white gown glide across the columns, a silk bell
that echoes down the long alley of pine and oak
where on her bridal day she walked beneath
a gold and silver tangle in the branches, a dust
the field slaves spread through the canopy of webs
hung by spiders her father shipped from Africa.

Now, under the snags of moss, a small wind
rises from that hollow of brick and cypress beams,
too weak to blow the ghosts away, though it carries
a bobwhite's call from the canebrake, the dry stalks
that rattle like chains, and from the worn earth it brings
a lolling odor of jasmine and black sweat.

What life do I betray, standing here
on the false side of history, facing two pasts
beyond approach: these ruins the moon will overflow
and, far behind, those sour cabins gone back to darkness
under the wild grass, the spearhead blades of palmetto?
Now, at the edge of judgment, I lean against
a rough pine stuck with locust pods split down the back,
and enter this long moment haunting the bottomland, a bitter
beauty that seven generations could not raze forever or restore.

Pilgrimage

Bootheels on the bottom rung, butt
Stuck on the barstool, and three beers
Past toting up these longneck empties—
Subtraction being my only numerate gift—
I'm talking to Fred of Fred's Lounge,

In Mamou, Louisiana, the two of us
Alone in the air-conditioned dark of afternoon:
That last sick fish in the bibs and gimme cap,
Red Man softening his jaw, has floundered
Back to the evils of the workday sun,
His coin still spinning, calling up
The frenzied French of some jukebox two-step
I couldn't hope to construe, even if both eyes
Were drained and level and locked in on
The same jars of pigs' feet and pickled egg.

I've angled down six states to hear
Fred unravel these yarns, legends of market Saturdays
When Revon Reed, microphone in the back booth
Rising from a mausoleum of dead Dixies, would open up
The Cajun caterwaul on KUEN, bare morning
And already the dance floor woozy with
A wash of alcohol, the waltz and the pigeonwing.
From the coulees and the cattle ranch, or the green
Spikes of rice in the flood fields, from the prairies
Of cotton and the flats of sugar cane, they come
In their weekend dresses and pressed pants—
Even that breadman stalled on his rounds, handing out
Warm samples of Evangeline Maid; and those teachers
Hired here from the motherland, their mission to
Purify the wayward tongue of Acadia; and the teenage atheist
Who dogs the daughters of the town cop and the chiropractor.

Fred sweats another brew across the grain, down payment
On the ticket I've reserved to Oblivion,
Window seat in the smoking car, ears still eager
As he whines away with his bayou haiku, his gumbo strut,
All the spice and license of the lowlands.
I've made this pilgrimage to leave my prints
On the pink beerocracy of cinderblock, to beard the ghosts
Of Arceneau and Fontenot and Thibodeaux,

Fiddles sizzling in a fat squall of accordion,
'Tit fer and guitars tingling through the tunes
Like skeeter drills in a trapline swamp, and on the roof
That tall antenna siphoning off to heaven
A case of this lubricated music, where the angels
Kick back on a cloud, their halos raked low,
Their lyres too lazy to keep up with
The syncopated spoons and the nubbly washboards,
As the band bears down on *Colinda* or covers
That mournful classic, *Hold My False Teeth*, making
Every molar this side of the Mississippi ache with gold.

There's no brassy hair at this quadrille;
In this stretch of the woods, no nymphettes in tube or tank top
Abrade the air with their bounceables; here,
No one guzzles from grief or self-defense. I've done
The Opelousas jitterbug at Slim's Y Kiki; I've been
To Boo-Boo's for the crawfish race, and killed
A Ville Platte moonjar at Snook's; but this room,
Sleepy as the single stoplight on Main Street,
Wakes in me an echo of its quickstep days,
Till I can almost hear that singer's catchweed call
And the froggy gargle of his *r*'s, and someone shouting
Don't drop the tater as the tune swings in.
You can still, in loose translation, pass a good time
At Fred's Lounge, in Mamou, Louisiana,
If Fred unwinds his tangled tales
And hoists another bottle to the bar, this one
On the house, his house, too many miles below
The one I've traveled from, a frozen outpost
In a foreign tribe, no chinaberry bush
Or bloody petals of Confederate rose, no spirits
Lifted to the shrine of pixilated grit.

Evening Services on North Rampart Street

You can waste your days and grace at the Easy Action
Or the Second Line Lounge, or chain yourself to the 8 ball
Snug in the pockets of the Auction Block (Ladies Invited and
    Respected),
Saving your soul on the layaway plan, no penance down,
Eternity to pay, and a last deal cut over the coffin,

Or you can come humbly to that church like a Legion Lodge,
Paint peeling from the slats and the stair rail, a homemade sign
Nailed up for the services: the Rev. Wyletta L. Pomroy presiding
At the Prince of Peace and Israel Baptized in the Southern Light.

They're testifying in their white robes and miters, the bishops and the
    brethren
And big women like angels with a thyroid problem, playing out
A cross-rhythm of the gospels on upright and drums, in one hand
The torch of a tambourine, and in the other, Jesus on a stick.

The Rev. Wyletta L. Pomroy calls up two legends from the dead:
That half-black, half-Mohawk singer from the Windy City,
Miss Leaf Anderson, who set this house in order, backed up
By her chorus of spirit guides, Queen Esther and Father Jones;
And Mother Catherine Seals, who always entered her Temple of
    Innocent Blood
Preaching feet-first from a hole in the roof, her mission there
To raise all the bastard babies of the neighborhood.

And before you feast at the laden tables, the long boards cramped
With a voodoo sampling of saints and candles, turkeys and cakes,
A star-spangled flag draped over the headdress of a hardwood chief,
Put yourself in the Rev.'s thick, prophetic hands, as the children do,
Dunked like doughnuts in a liquid grave, then spun dry in a spasm,
A trance with the gowns belled out, eyes burning from the body's dark.

Edified at the altar, sanctified in the tank, tongue taking on
The voice of John the Revelator, the grunts of Sitting Bull,
You'll turn from bad liquor to the Lord, and feel that spark
As if you'd touched a live wire let down from heaven:
A soul in shock: ghost on a pinwheel in the voltage dance.

The Weaning

It starts with little things—
a blue web belt from the navy,
a book of the greatest chess games,
a boy scout knife with ten blades.
You suspect that this time
they have not been lost, or mislaid, or left somewhere,
but subtracted,
that something has begun
erasing,
like ciphers, like tracks,
the curios of your history
starting back at the first
and gaining on you every day.
When you begin to miss certain people,
you know the house itself is next
or the street of green trees.
One morning when you wake it will be
color
and you will wander for days in snow
before, suddenly, even the whiteness goes.
But by then it will be
just one more thing.

Anniversary

1

It's hard to believe you've missed my wife
and your grandson, twenty-five years of fishing
and funny movies.
Every day you sleep
past breakfast, past supper.

What are you listening to
down in your room, your head
tilted toward the dark?
What dream is so beautiful it cannot spare you?

2

Soon I'll be the age you are
forever, the day you pulled
off the interstate, your heart
boiling like a cracked block,
to die in a phone booth
while everyone passed you by.

We'll be twins—
I see us coming in the amber of store windows.
The next day I'll be
the eldest, you
tagging along to some
place you've already been.

Already you could be my mother's son.
Someday you could be mine.
Maybe then you'd listen
when I told you to stay
off the fatty foods and the interstates,
to slow down and stay well.
To grow old. To call.

Men as Trees Walking

I learned early what that verse
meant, "For now we see as through a glass
darkly." My mother wouldn't buy me any
glasses because then I'd be a foureyes,

maybe even play in the band like the rest
of the pansies, or like my father, polishing
his lenses, head bent, hands
before his face as if
praying, no football
hero. Teachers tired of my leaning
in from the front row, chalk dust in
my hair, begged her in notes: like the blind
man in the Bible miracle, he sees men
as trees, and trees as lime
jello. Going out for passes, I was
lost like the end of the world when
everybody running sees the sky but me.
The coach threw his hat in the dust: "Son,
have you *ever* caught a pass?" I never
did, but when she gave in, let me have
my specs, it was like heaven, she even more
beautiful with wrinkles, people gross
as bears now limber as hickory, spare
as willows. And the trees, firmed up,
erect at last, were like emerald fish with each
scale whole and succinct, as if they would never
ever drop a leaf, or a pass.

LEE MEITZEN GRUE

Christmas

It falls like a sash weight
between Thanksgiving and Mardi Gras.

Fogged by my own breath
a cold window clouds the heavy green
draining the elephant ears.
Everything is down on the root—wet,
even the roaches in their little dirt cribs are paddling.

A walk past St. Louis No. 2,
where bodies float in their sunken tubs,
somebody's Christmas is there piled on an ash heap:
padded sateen crosses, burnt wires like crown-studded
thorns to pierce flowers, remains of a pink sash.

Oh, you hangers of stockings, pinecone gatherers, tree choppers,
curlers of ribbons, writers of checks,
Santa Claus is sleeping under the too green grass,

and I am girding my loins for happiness,
like the skinny man
with the goosepimpled butt in the stall
at the bus station, knowing
it is momentary, spasmodic—hard
to keep up.

Give me the children's list.
What do they need?
I can tell you
you can't get it at Zayre's, K-Mart, or J. C. Penny.
You can't get it for more money at Hausmann's
or at Sak's for plastic.
Every year they praise it on cards,
but nobody's got the price, the ticket,
or even a clue.

This is the wrap-up
in pretty paper: The rain has stopped,
tires lick at the wet pavement,
go up into a dark garage,
where I go down the elevator
to the first floor of D. H. Holmes.
The candy counter is chocolate in gold and red foil,
the perfumes are lolling around fat-bottled
smoking exotic oils,
behind the counters are women in Monteil masks,
I go up to them to get what I can,
cheap.

Babe Stovall on a Bare Stage

at the Quorum Club: 1963

in suspenders and a
blue bebop hat.
    C. C. Rider . . .
    Oh, see what you done done
    You made me love you now your man done come,

face, irregular and reseamed,
like a pair of old jeans,
eyes yellow to the core,
repeats of sneaky pete . . . thunderbird and muscatel.

On the Square, Babe the street musician
says,
        Pass the bottle,
to a shaky guitar man.
Drinks out of a brown paper bag
in the city of the go-cup.

Babe keens where he comes from, Mississippi,
his band, two guitars and a washtub,
at a no-pay party
for friendship . . . drinks,
sings about Brown so she's a color and a woman,
picks steel guitar dirt farm
for a bunch of dropouts
who sop up brotherhood like it's gravy
with *No War* like it's cornbread,

twenty-year-olds on the floor, parents
of a newborn . . .
spoons, beer cans, and *Don't*
       wake the baby in the next room,
plays
as if they—we—can learn where he's been,
see what he's seen,
his raspy voice
strains cords in his neck like
hemp at a lynching, but that wasn't
what his music was. . . .
It was a spread table,
all we had to do was eat.

Valentine

A man stands
in the shower ruminating
like a dumb animal
in the rain, and something awful
on the edge of thought
lurches out of the gray hair on his chest,
slides down the face of his body
to clog up the drain
like the label off a bottle of shampoo.

Has the old pumperoo that puffed up the stairs
ceased wheezing? No, it wants
to say: my heart is heavy,
    my heart aches,
    wants to be a cinnamon red-hot, sticky and sweet,
    to be red-slick paper in a neat envelope,

but no Valentine, no seat of feeling anymore.
He thinks:
        Better to hold on to this hollow
        that roars at night
        like the sea in a vacant shell than to
        replace the pump
        with something small, artificial, beastly, or worse,
        something human.

WILLIAM HATHAWAY

Horse Sense

I

One after another, down the cement alley
under high dangling bulbs ablaze with halo
but faint light, I threw open their stall screens.
In the darkness I could hear their stamps
and soft splutters as they awoke from green
dreams. At my whistle the sudden rumble
arose, confused crashes from that scramble
shaking the great tin sheets. Cocked
tails flickered up from massive buttocks
into those long faces whose wild nodding
made eyes gleam white arcs for the thunder.

They must have seen a small shadow,
so squat and black in a vast square
of silver heaven as they snorted and chortled
out to me, pushing the smell of horse ahead
of them. And steaming and wheezing on
the frozen yard they rubbed their fat, rough
tongues on my head, jostled me to snow-
banks, nosed me everywhere for fruit
and sugar. Untucked and undone, sprawled on
ice, I was helpless with laughter, too weak
for breath, under their moist, quivering nostrils.

Merry eyes: I was drunk off the whiff of their
sweat, on the rhythmic turmoil of muscle
and hoof. Bright light in the morning.

II

I pole-fished the meadow pond in mid-
summer with my towheaded children.
Hey, this was supposed to be fun!

But too white and soft for the glare, their
cheeks over-ripened fast and their washed
blue eyes grew lidded from heat and tedium.
The pecan tree, our only shade, fairly
dripped with bitter tannin and from
crushed weeds the still air reeked sweet
and sour with dusts, pollens, chlorophyll
and rank herbal acids. All and everywhere
they touched made an itch, and unseen
but often felt insects pitched fierce drones.

But it was the horses my kids feared most;
the curious pony who cantered in close
sideways, to grunt and paw the grass.
Sun flashed off his slick flanks and when
he grinned his huge yellow teeth sent
them clutching at my legs, trembling pillars
of a cursed city. Against these woes
their choral whine rose in stridency,
in the face of my disdain, until nothing
remained but to clean the catch and go.

Putting the knifepoint in the black anus
to slice up the milky belly to the throat,
robin's breast–sunrise orange, I glanced
at the small knees grouped around me
then higher into a silent gaze of disgust.
Their eyes on my sequined, gory hands
were as blank as when they recoiled from
the viscous saliva roping the old mare's
mouth. Too small to phrase it for themselves;
I asked instead: Was this cruelty born in me
or did I learn? It is long past memory.

I led my wife's children around the mines
of mahogany turds, back to the baking car.

III

On famous Bourbon Street I saw old nags
hooked to tourist buggies, parked in full
sun. Yellow mucus dripped from slack
mouths to the recycled cobbles of that
adult disneyland for deviants, and often
I saw fetlocks matted with oozing scabs
and flies preening their resplendent faces
in a paradise of open sores. Too humid
for prolonged rage, too overwhelmed
by sordid sight to pity any but myself,
I hid in the ersatz cool of an unlit bar.
Even there I heard the driver croak "Ya-
hoo!" and that forlorn clop-clop
fade into city sounds like memories
ringing back so vague you feel the cells
give a final pop and give up sense for good.

My father tended a horse like that.
While his father quoted scripture
by the hour to customers, he sat
on the wagon seat, lost in great books.
That patient beast knew the route,
the way home, and how to stamp
for oats. My father's body sat sentry
over the inventory, while his mind
stormed Troy, or led white Bucephalus
out of a cool glade onto Persian plains.

Like a Gift this vision, more real than
the cruel streets, took me in the Absinthe Bar:
Father high on his perch in brown knickers,
his eyes drinking the words, the slightest
twitching of lips, while around the whole cast
glowed a profound calmness of horse

and I arose from the untasted whiskey,
eager for the road, eager for new pastures
where horses browsed in shadows of oil tanks.

The Poet Hunts Doves with the Natchitoches Police

for Jim Dyson

A man's handle is Polar Bear and he
asks for Roughneck's ten-twenty.
It is seven thirty, hungover
and crushed in the cab of a pick-up.
So many fantastic dials and gauges!
Jimmy calls himself Pervert over
the thick highway air to Roughneck.
If asked to speak I would be
Captain Video—"Video" for short.

We ease down into the soft brown field,
awhir with hidden creatures, load up
shotguns and squat in high weeds to wait.
Doves sail over alone, in pairs, in threes,
like fighter planes lost from formation.
Sharp reports, puffs of feathers, a bit-
ter rain of pellets and often everywhere
that high halloo "Doves, boys, doves!"
My own hands darken with blood.

I never knew how easy it is to shoot,
and hit. I try to think of Turgenev
but only *Field & Stream* in a dentist's
office will surface. The wounded bird
hops ahead as I try to gun-butt it dead.
"Hey New York, this ain't no golf course."
The voice of God from out of the brush.

There in the truck's bed mounds of gray
dead, beyond the limits of law or sense.
Sour whiskey finally at peace in my belly,
accepted as friend, finally, when all is said
and done. The smell is nothing and we
save the tiny red hearts with the fleshy
breasts to eat. More whiskey to burn
out the feather tickling in the throat,
to ease the violence of the night, to
celebrate the loneliness of being men.

Driving to Work

Smacker in the ditch.
Smackim too. Smackem
Jack'n Jills headoverheels /
assoverteakettle down
into the running grave
and lettem therein grin
empty-eye upto empty sky.
Teachem onceinferall
not to jogin the fuckenroad.
Jeslookitem. Humpty-
dump, humpty-dump—cheek-
to-cheek. Secret cracks
sliding upendown slicksweat
sweet in spandex. O sleek
as antelope do my betters
lope. Rightthru hazy dead
waterwiggling outta asphalt
like veils of tears
smearinup roadside sights
us workinstiffs creep light
by light by—late
to slambang jobsofwork.

AVA LEAVELL HAYMON

Fence

Say you're in kindergarten
and your teacher tells you draw a fence.
The black crayon's thick as another thumb,
you have to bear down with your whole arm.
You mash crayon marks
against the paper, one at a time,
and the construction paper
begins to move under your hands,
scrolling off a giant roll
she didn't tell you about.
Say you're determined to do it right
and you don't get bored and
the paper's no problem
since it just keeps coming
and you go on for a couple of years,
picket after picket, the lines
getting straighter while your fingers
grow a little, thin down, and curl
around the crayola
which is now a yellow pencil
and you're scratching out
an earnest outline of skinny rectangles,
like teeth, and you've invented
the second dimension, although you don't know
to call it that, and you keep on
doing teeth for a while and the faithful
slow-moving paper gets blue lines on it
like 3-hole notebook sheets except
it's this assembly line belt that
just keeps rolling and rolling and
the teeth get straighter—
more like piano keys—and say you're taller
and have to stoop over the paper a little,
which is good drawing paper now, no blue lines,

and you feel a callus bumping up
on your third finger and your chest's
getting bumpy, too, and you look out
the classroom window at a fence
and your fine muscles knit in
another dimension—the sides of your boards
crease and fold back and you sketch them
that way for some time and even
the little point on the top
gets a side, and you look up again and now
a crosspiece drags its way along,
peeking between slats.
Then the teacher nods, and
says you can go to algebra.

But say if you kept on—if the teacher forgot
you were in there all by yourself
with the moving paper and the instructions
to get it right. And say you kept on
till you gazed at the fence outside
every time before you looked down to sketch,
and once you saw one of the slats
out there in full sun open like a hole melting
in a filmstrip and a dazzling light sizzles
out of it, and you look back down quick
but now the slats you are drawing
start to gape into holes in the sliding paper,
holes that sear open under your hands and a light
brighter than the classroom fluorescent
you've been under so long, brighter
than the glare out the window on
the white picket fence, brighter than anything
—say those holes burn open
in the paper you're so used to and
that light underneath comes through.

The Holy Ghost Goes Out for Little League

The outfield—just the place for him!
The "vast outfield" Lefty Gomez
credited with his success.
He imagined it matched
his spaciousness, his inability
to touch base, to stay within lines.

The high pop fly rising toward him
warmed him to ecstasy in the laws of motion
—that pull toward an object he could never know.
It floated out patient as planets,
amber and gold from the late afternoon sun,
the crack of ash just slower than the ball.

He saw two earths, wrapping their separate flights
in sweeping lines of gravity
and then the little leather baseball
would plummet right through him
—grapeshot through flame—
and thump in the way of all real things
against the grass near the fence.

Sighting

I plan to stare at the horizon all day,
to relax my neck, let go my old griefs.
But the sloshing surf drags down my eyes,
provokes a squawl of gulls, undermines
the castles of loudmouth boys. Sand and sunscreen
crawl in my sweaty suit. And lovers promenade,
rubbed over every tanned inch with coconut oil or Panama Jack,
the huge sea behind them soupstock of their own desire.

I try again. My eyes, lifted into the glare,
sting from last night's piña coladas, salt swim.
The planet rim I have in mind smudges in a Gulf haze.

I squint for distance: the farthest waves draw my eyes,
running off the world curve in a shudder. I see
whale bodies roll over, impossible in scale that far off.
Then the earth leans away to India or China,
becomes a map, and I have lost my place again.

There is no line, I cannot fix it.
No Rubicon where ions, having enough of sea
or filling enough with sun, leap for and become sky.
These rowdy sand engineers must draw it when they go
home to school: beach and ocean a double stripe—
yellow, green crayola on construction paper.
Sky, a layer of stiff blue wax, rubbed hard
across the very top of the page.

Down the strand, three brown pelicans pop into flight,
straight off threatened species' lists, homilies for Mother's Day.
Sure enough, there are the unselfish gabble throats,
the martyred breasts, swollen feet from Audubon prints.
They wingbeat low in a tight unison, all dull feather
and hollow bone creaking above sunbathers in bright lycra,
trace the water's hissing edge—with unpredicted grace—
and finally out of sight.

Epithalamium

Call me psychic. All I can
tell you is, I knew it wasn't
mine. Or was, actually, only I wasn't myself,
and if I wasn't there, how could I be held to account?
There, I mean, in flesh, maybe. . . . The march
starting, everyone straining around to watch me where
ere I walked, me standing petrified,
literally, in The Dress and I'm thinking
I can't do this. I must have said it out loud
for his sister and aunt hissed *Yes, you can,*
and pushed me out to sea. I swam down
into my future, released for the last time from my father,
shocked as Lazarus. And if my vow sounded
as clear as a Tibetan bowl, it's because I was
as mindless and molded and empty as one,
chanting Yes yes yes whatever you say I do.

A Romance

When the thieves struck,
they brought a casserole,
which they popped in the oven
while they cleaned the place out.
It was bubbling when the owners returned
to find a bottle of white wine chilling,
the aroma of their meal,
and not much else.
Of course there was no silver or china
on which to dine, but the thieves
had left a table, two chairs
and the bed.

                   How
thoughtful, the wife said.
Indeed, sighed the husband.

They picked glass from the shattered window,
slivered it into the salad,
scooped the casserole
with a few odd spoons left them.
It reminded them of their first
                            years together
when life had seemed so uncluttered.
They licked each other's fingers
since the napkins were misplaced.
They clinked the wine bottle
with the milk bottle for future luck.
They both agreed that romance
was back in their lives.

Turtle Soup at Mandina's

Gobs of meat knobbed with fat sink below my spoon.
The waiter sweeps a fifth of sherry past my nose.
The surface doused, "And more?" he asks, one eye on the next
table, crumpled bills, dead crabs sprawled on plates.
I want more, and more, the sherry clears a window
on the grease like ice on a filthy pond.
I was so hungry when I read the words, "Turtle Soup."

I swirl the sherry, it melts like salve in a wound.
A world swirls below my spoon, and a muddy river
winds through the broth, past the old Confederate statuary
and the telescope bright with Jupiter by the Cafe du Monde,
past the hooker in a leopardskin bikini with a tiger tattoo,
past Port of Call and Charmaine Neville clearing notes
in the smoky air, past bottles smashed on Charity,
past Jules Acer the chess master in his red beret,
past the Jackson Square shoeshine, past I-10 out of here
past a green shack in the marsh with a waterfront porch
past the turtles lazy as rocks who sun their black shells
and drop in the muck if you as much as breathe
only to float up out of the murk in bits and pieces
at the bottom of my spoon. Oh generous broth, disgust
is the birthplace of taste, delicious New Orleans turtle soup.

A Construction of Clouds

He rises perfectly into the sky
a young god with a talent
for suffering on behalf of others.

Four hundred years stripped away
Raphael's yellow Jesus is in the pink
a Transfiguration fresh as doubt.

At his back a jumbo cloud billows
hospital white, its x-rayed brilliance
"a stunning feat of restoration"

or so the museum poster claims.
Whatever is holy evaporates, I think
weeks later as a wet sundown

paints a lawn of flies, twitching
of cow tails and horse behinds
and quotes a sky of Raphael originals

for our unvarnished Baton Rouge.
We peer into a mist that wipes the levee
like a damp rag. Will some god come

to rescue us, restore our faded daydreams
to their true colors? The sky divides
into swimming pools of silver and green.

It is an amazing weather that
builds a palace of clouds high
as the eye can climb then sends it

tumbling down like a child's blocks
with adult croaks of thunder
to punctuate the shape of things to come.

The building of clouds is on the rise
knock them down who will, the bright
flashes of their tumbling, the equal rain.

The Mermaid Story

It was one of the lesser fairy tales:
a mermaid rescued a drowning prince,
swam him to shore, then pined away
because she missed the weight of him

and the heat of his breath against her neck,
nothing at all like the trickle of cool
saltwater flushed from delicate gills
when she kissed the mermen back in school.

But since there are witches underwater
as well as over, within a year
she'd bargained away her tail for legs;
and her tongue, too, as legs were dear.

She married the prince. His body hair
tickled like beachgrass parched in sun.
An eel grew where his legs forked:
she couldn't tell this to anyone.

Back in the anti-universe,
a human woman with two tongues
rooted to the floor of her mouth
like anemones has just swum

so deep with her freak tail,
her head spins and the sea goes black.
We'll see if the tongue she bargained for
can send a message back.

Mardi Gras Parade

Shy as I am, my arms fly out
To every man in costume tossing beads.

I do not beg, as a rule,
But even the gray-gloved winter trees

Have their fingers out, and the children around me
Pounce on doubloons with tennis shoes
Like street tapdancers on pocket change.
I do not beg, except from you.

Maybe you're here with your wife and daughters,
Crabby, thinking the car is parked
Illegally, and won't be there
When you walk back to it after dark,

Swinging the jumbled treasure bags,
Long after I have watched and gone:
You are the jewels out of reach in those branches,
I am the branches they snag upon.

Richard Katrovas

Black English

How to say the distance, not the difference,
is the problem.
In her Freshman composition
Shellanda writes that most men
treat cars better than they treat women,
describes her brother rubbing
wax for hours
into red-washed steel and blinding chrome;

she is hilarious and tactful implying
the absurdity of his erotic care, and suggesting
he loves women only in his dreams.

I imagine Shellanda's brother cruising
St. Charles on a Friday night, easing
his bright machine past the homes of wealthy whites.
There is no bitterness in his face, no wonder,
only the self-satisfaction of a young man
who keeps what he owns looking nice.

Maybe at home he's one mean bastard.
But on the rich strip at night just driving
and looking around, listening to loud
music and not judging, not judging
even himself, he feels the TV
in his brain click off when the soft
white of a trolley's headlamp—
blocks away—seems a false though lovely
offering for which words will not do,

and do not matter.

Sky

On the first cool day in half a year,
an October Sunday in New Orleans,
I waken happy in my new house.
You know, sunlight, breezes, bells,
coffee, thick newspaper, all that.
When I shuffle out to walk my little dog
there's a kid, fourteen maybe,
staring down and holding his dark face
in his dark hands, on the stoop
of the abandoned house next door.
His shoes are torn and cruddy;
his filthy shirt is blooming
from his back pocket; his bony torso
is ashy black and sunken. Why do I think
in childhood he wept violently and often,
that he'll spend his adolescence
constructing alternatives to weeping,
just one of which is to sit alone
in breezy morning sunlight
and dream himself beyond the dull,
fixed circumstances of his life?
My brain is glossy with the world's news,
my heart aglow with sugar and caffeine.
All over town citizens are praying or plotting,
sleeping late or taking stock.
He looks at me and mumbles he's just resting,
which means don't worry, White Bread,
I won't smash your Ford or rape your dog
or steal your VCR, just don't worry.
Drag your silly puff around the block
and disappear. Today, this hour,
I am meant for this stoop. This air
I breathe is mine all mine, this sunlight
and sputter of tiny breezes just for me.
I'm hungry, but that's okay, for now.
For now, we are quiet in the flat regard

with which we hold each other; he drops his head
once more and I walk on, recalling hunger,
the unspeakable passions it engenders,
the ugly, useless wisdom of it.
With tainted sadness I remember such
as all the elegant systems
I've since peered upon will never steel
against the acid fact of physical despair,
but when I turn and trot my little love
back home to face the kid again, to speak
to him not like a father, but to ask
him into my house to eat, he is blocks away.

The Surfer

> Father, you needn't punish me anymore.
> I shall punish myself now.
>
> —Sigmund Freud

Cold April ocean thrilled the surfer's skin
And shocked his brain alert; graphing the flow,
The first full minute after he'd sliced in,
Undulating upon the drift below
The shifting drifts of salty morning air,
He (serpentine) stared out at the charmed swells,
Forgot mere physics of how they could tear
White dripping roots that blurred to green then fell
To curling spread of aqua-smooth release.
That storied movement was destination.
Like one issued grim orders to police
A turbulent range defining nations,
Between the gray, brake-boulders at his lee
And a thin, sweeping sandbar, he shuttled
Parallel, as grieving to memory.

Sensation palpable as passion pulled
A part of him passion was not meant to reach,
The quiet, dry center where balance gripped
His spine, grapneled his will onto the beach.
A buoy frigged upon the line where currents ripped
A quarter mile beyond where breakers rise.
He'd seen a tourist paddle out that far
To dumb-show for a lover, then heard the cries,
High rasps of terror diminished in air
Weighted with the ocean's contrabass.
Sex and dancing define repetition
In lyric terms of mirroring and pace.
This is what he does, what must be done,
When doing must be felt so he may feel.
Others waken to their dread and live it;
Dreading life, he wakens squatting in the peel
Of water pushing water to a limit
His mother voiced in pain when he was born.
His longest ride he always dreams his last.
Young men look back upon themselves and mourn
Futures in repetitions that are past.

From the French Market

Cinnamon ladies
in gingham bonnets
and white aprons
singing their *fleurs,*
calas or ginger cakes,
sitting on the banquettes
or walking under the eaves
of the Indian Market amid
Misu's, Herrmeisters, Chiefs,
and thieves, in their butter-soft
Creole language:
"Calas, tout chaud!"
or in Spanish:
"Flores, gardénias, jasmin"
or in French:
"Petit gâteaux, pralines,"

whatever the visitor should please.

These *marchandes* would save
picayunes enough to one day
buy a sister or a son or
herself. Did Madame know
that every praline bought
meant a sweeter step to
liberty for one so hated?
That even though the sun boiled
hot, and painful blood clots
formed on heavy legs from
walking, standing, that through
days of rain and mud and heavy
fevered air that caught them
short of breath and sick-
weary they remained?

That they became fixed as
present-day stuffed Mammy Dolls,
big as life and still the butt
of horrid jokes that belie what
dignity crowned that checkered
rag, that Creole kerchief, *tignon*,
mandated by law to hide their beauty,
mammy rag, nigger rag, dolls, play-
things, souvenirs?

Those earring hoops were made of
gold. Thick painted lips were
actually Senegalese small and
not rouged.
Bulging eyes were quite
proportioned, varied in color,
quick and clever.
And in that melodic speech
she was sure to answer your
vileness or evil and hurl curses
from old gods against you or
your progeny if you troubled her.

Oh, I would fear this caricature
despite her contorted face.
And do not mean her ill with back-
ward glance or words. Her anger,
now more than two centuries old,
could send a plague, a killer storm,
or something unexplained and in the
very air.

Thibodaux

The Massacre of November 22, 1887

Surely there was also the warmth
of "Für Elise" from a piano, and

a noble-voiced soprano raised
"He Leadeth Me" for next Sunday's
sermon. There must have been
cotton lace in the making by
brown hands unaware of distant
danger, and the first cooing
laugh of a newborn caught by
eyes of surprised parents. Someone
must have baked a sweet potato pie
for aunt and uncle, married fifty
years; and someone must have blenched
at the roar of whispered hate, those
sins of indifference.

When the first shots were fired, as
the striking cane workers, the Creoles
who led them were hacked with machetes,
as death lay on the road, bloated the
river, rustled the frost on the trees,
surely someone wept like raging rain.

Tales of panic, tales of fear from
hiding the strikers, tales of lynchings
and worse stunted this town. The Knights
of Labor lost its cause, its core. Those
who did not die went back to the fields
for seven dollars a month; any wounded
Creoles fled forever. Planters' mansions
huddled, crumbled, most, like the Confederacy,
would struggle and fall.

Thibodaux sits small, perhaps a little lonely
in its sylvan landscape. There are no Creoles
of color here, but there are people like you,
Mary Morton, who by their wisdom, bravely
harbor true southern kindness; and those of us
who fear the present past may breathe free and
for a while, forgive.

La Chaudrière Pélé La Grègue . . .

He, Cajun.
Et toi, Créole,
Cofaire to pélé to même
Blanc ou Noir? Qui donnein toi noms-yé?
Nous tous descendants des Francais, Espagnols,
Africains, Indiens, Acadians, Haitiens,
Et tout z'autres Gombo People qui té vinir à
La Louisiane. Epice-yé té fait le Gombo.
Nous culture riche servi comme nous liaison commun.
Nous sommes du même sang-paprika et
Sang-là joindre nous avec le monde.
Si racistes-yé oulé mettre le'étoiles de papier
Sur nous lapeau pour dire nous ça nous yé.
Laizzez-yé bouillir dans la merde.
C'est nous—les franco-louisianais, fiers de
Nous l'Héritage Francais et Africain. C'est nous—
Européen, Africain, Asiatique et Américain.
Cajun, Créole. Annons êt fier pour dire ça.
Tant pis pour tout-ça-yé qui pas laimein ça
Nous yé. Comment longtemps yé péut garder nous
Et dire nous, nous pas éxiste?
Mais mon ami, pas garrochez l'épice
Parce que li trop blanc ou trop noir.
Si vous fait ça, to sa pas gain Gombo
Jamain plus, mais un ragout fondu salé-là
Fait avec la chair niée de to l'ancestre-yé,
To grandmère, to grandpère, to mère, to père,
To soeur, to frère, to tante, to nonc,
To cousin, to niece, to nevèu, to pitits, ou
To-même.

The Pot Calls the Coffeepot . . .

Hey, Cajun,
And you, Creole,
How come you call yourself
White or Black? Who gave you these names?
We are descendants of the French, the Spanish,
The African, the Indian, the Acadian, the Haitian, and
All the other Gombo People who came to
Louisiana. These spices made the Gombo.
Our rich culture serves as our common bond.
We are of the same paprika blood, and that
Blood connects us with the world.
If racists want to stick paper stars on our
Skins to tell us what we are, let them
Boil in hell with their foolishness.
We are the Louisiana French, proud of
The French and African heritage. We are
European, African, Asian, and American.
Cajun, Creole. Let us dare to say it.
And so much the worst for those who do not like
What we are. How long can they look at us and tell
Us we do not exist?
But my friend, do not throw away the spice
Because it is too light or too dark.
If you do that you will not have Gombo
Ever again, but a foul melted stew made up of
The denied flesh of your ancestors,
Your grandmother, your grandfather, your mother,
Your father, your sister, your brother,
Your aunt, your uncle, your cousin, your niece,
Your nephew, your children or
Yourself.

DAVID KIRBY

Ode to Languor

My father and I are watching the opera *Susannah*,
       or at least I am, for my father has fallen
into a deep and dreamless slumber, the way

he always has—when I was young, he used
       to take me to the *National Geographic* film
series on Wednesdays, and once,

as the Mud Men of New Guinea were shaking
       their spears at the camera, Johnny Taylor
(I was too self-conscious to sit with

anyone not my age) nudged me and said,
       "Look at that old man sleeping!" Forty
years later, I am almost an old man myself

and grateful for the quality of languor,
       almost certainly genetically transmitted.
Blessed parent! He is also the perfect

erotic role model, i.e., not. My father
       chased no skirts—after a while,
not even my mother's. When I think of

friends who have broken their hearts
       in the pursuit of unattainable women,
I am all the more grateful to my drowsy father.

Keats praised languor: easeful death was something
       he was more than half in love with,
though he didn't mean a passing like his own.

Keats wanted a death-in-art, a rich death,
       with a nightingale pouring forth its soul
as Susannah, wronged by the lustful elders,

pours forth hers, my eyes closing,
       my head bending toward that
of my dreamless father, this good man sleeping.

The Potato Mash
   (More Indefinite and More Soluble)

If Debussy had written the score to the story of my adolescence,
   he would have called it, after the name of the poem
by his good friend Mallarmé, *L'Après-Midi d'un Dope.*
   So many adventures! All of them stupid.
For a while I worked for a rock band;
   I handled the bookings, the equipment, and the snacks.
The band leader played the French horn,
   which is all he knew how to play;
it was the only rock-and-roll French horn in the business.

   And the bassist, who had never played at all,
just hit whatever notes he felt like hitting,
   saying it didn't make any difference
because nobody ever paid any attention to the bass line anyway.
   Then there were the two blind brothers,
a drummer and a guitarist,
   good musicians who drank bourbon and ate doughnuts
during the shows, always with disastrous results,
   though the band was horrible to begin with.

We never accomplished our goal of meeting pliant women,
   and everywhere we went,
the drunken fishermen we played for were mad at us
   because our music had not brought out any women for them.
Instead we played songs like "The Mashed Potatoes,"
   each time to a smaller and surlier crowd.
We "loosened classical tonality" the way Debussy did,
   and at times we destroyed it, like Schoenberg,
when the blind boys were too far gone.

   Our last night, I knew it was going to be bad;
one of the customers had stopped me coming back
   from the men's room to ask why I didn't use hair tonic.
Then a big guy in suspenders and a plaid shirt
   and a cap that said "Sex is like snow,
you never know how many inches you're going to get"
   came up to the bandstand and asked,

———

"Y'all can play dat Potato Mash?"
    We knew our career was over anyway,

so we began to laugh and make fun of him,
    and he and his friends jumped up on stage
to throw beer at us and turn over the drum kit.
    The three of us who could see were frightened
by these hairy bayou men with their great hard bellies
    and their forearms big as Popeye's,
but the blind boys didn't give a shit
    and were ripped on bourbon and doughnuts anyway;
howling, their fish-belly eyes red in the light

    from the beer signs, the blind boys lashed out
and began to hit the men and us and each other
    with the neck of the guitar and the drum sticks.
It was a fight in hell: "The Musicians versus the Fishermen,"
    like a myth from some country that had never developed
much of a culture. I got a cut lip and my first real hangover,
    and for days my parents heaped shame on my silent head.
But it was worth it to have seen the blind boys
    whip the ass of those tough fishermen;

for sure, they did the Potato Mash. Later we got more bourbon
    and more doughnuts and had a real party. We sang and threw up,
and one of the blind boys cried for his mother.
    That was our only good moment—our last. On the ride home,
we were a lyrical and pantheistic group of fellows,
    and our music was *plus vague et plus soluble dans l'air*,
according to the formula of the poet Verlaine,
    son-in-law of Madame Mauté de Fleurville,
Debussy's first teacher and herself a student of Chopin.

YUSEF KOMUNYAKAA

Lingo

Herodotus, embroiled in his story,
    tells how the Phoenicians lent
        war fleets to Greece

& Egypt, how a flotilla
    eased like salmon in birth water
        & sailed the Red Sea,

hoping to circumnavigate Africa
    around the Cape of Good Hope
        & along Gibraltar. A blue

door opening. Diodorus
    says of the Ethiopians
        that "born under the sun's path,

its warmth may have ripened them
    earlier than other men." As if
        a ventriloquist inherited

the banter of a sailor's parrot,
    words weave with Herodotus's—
        angel food . . . sellers didn't touch

the gold . . . devil's food. The stories
    become flesh as these ghosts
        argue about what's lost

in translation, believing two images
    should spawn & ignite a star
        in the eyes of a sphinx

or soothsayer. Sometimes they do.
    There's a reason why the dead
        talk through a medium

about how Aryans drove cattle
along the seven rivers & left
dark-skinned Dravidians

with tongues cut out. Sugarcane
fields burning. The holy air
smelling of ghee & soma.

These ghosts know that the power
of suggestion is more than body
language: white list, black

sheep, white tie, black market.
Fear climbs the tribal brainstem
or wills itself up an apple tree,

hiding from the dream animal
inside. The serpent speaks
like a Lacan signifier,

posing as a born-again agrarian
who loves computer terminals
better than cotton blossoms.

The hidden agenda isn't a woman
or man, is it? Language seduces
& repels. The fraternal seed is

planted, then we wail to reap
whirlwind & blessing. Each prefix
clings like a hookworm

inside us. If not the split-tongued
rook, then the sparrow is condemned
to sing the angel down.

Mud

She works in the corner of the porch
Where a trumpet vine crawls up to falling
Light. There's always some solitary
Bridge to cross. Right hand

& left hand. The dirtdobber
Shapes a divided cell
Out of everything she knows,
Back & forth between the ditch.

I could take a stick & play
God. Soldier. Sadist. Nosing
Mud into place, she hums the world's
Smallest motor. Later, each larva

Quivers like bait on a hook . . . spermatozoa
Clustered in a song of clay. So small
Only the insignificance can begin
To fill the afternoon.

Double Exposure

Wing-footed Perseus
 slays the Gorgons,
  wearing his helmet

of midnight, beheaded Medusa,
 & the gods are pleased.
  Sometimes a daydream

frees a man into the sky.
 Queen Cassiopeia boasts
  that she's more gorgeous

than the daughters of Nereus.
 But the gods are revengeful;
  they want her daughter

sacrificed to a serpent.
     The Ethiopians are devoured
          by the hundreds, till

her father, Cepheus,
     says Yes. Beautiful
          Andromeda lies chained

to a rocky ledge by the sea.
     But wing-footed Perseus
          sees her & falls

in love. After he slays
     the sea serpent, they
          marry & sail to Greece.

More than a thousand years
     away, I laugh, thumbing
          through a book of photographs

on the history of rock
     & roll: white dancers
          separated from blacks

by a rope down the center
     of the club, twisting to
          rhythm & blues.

PINKIE GORDON LANE

Baton Rouge

Horizontal
this city spreads herself
like a great cat sprawled
in the sun.

Her sounds are sponged into
the overhanging sky
that measures her dimensions
by tips of sweet gums
breaking the horizon,
by tar-black smoke
(from its monstrous oil plant)
belched from fierce
hissing streaks
of orange fire.

Sweet rain-soaked air
drips from her belly's
felt need
and the summer's sun
vaporizes the tears
of her ever present
poor.

Traveling by car transports
to green plains
and purple bayous:
cypresses moss-strung
and drooping to wedged base
split by gray waters
carrying the face of day
and cradling the stillness
of nights.

The city spins . . .
simulating metropolis

flops back on her boneless
tail
and purrs
herself
to ambiance.

Migration

The winter birds
are flying from the North
to embrace our swamps,
our rain-trapped fields.
My backyard trees hang
heavy and Louisiana
is a depot for this alien flock.
Their noisy forms slice the air
in restless flight
translated out of need.

The autumn mist mudpacks
the earth. Caladiums,
their once firm stalks
reaching high, now bend
to snake the grass and wait
for death. Hibiscus
forks the air to reach
the sky—a last count
before frost. I know

the time to seek
new ground, when what
I wanted, felt, erupts
from leaning's desert ice,
flocks to a new spring
and southern warmth—

winter's frost a forgotten
land, and time a revolving
flame.

I Never Scream

> Remember this: I never scream . . .
>
> —May Miller

The hour draws its own design
on this thin atmosphere
floating like lint outside my window.
That quick black pattern
of branches abstracts
the green canvas of leaves.
And the puddle at the base
spacing the ground
in spots of sky-reflected light
lacks the depth to shape
my mind.

I have a locked-in psyche,
leather-padded, hinged,
opening up and thrusting out
only when I choose
to make it so.

I am weather bound
insulated
cooled by laminated shadows
closing out harshness
locking in brief hushed
colors of sound.

I see the patterns
as they design

the not impetuous night.
Do they reach the point
where space meets space
where twilight spans the mind
in one broad thrust—
in a warm, soft band
melting, flowing,
gone?

MARTHA MCFERREN

Why I Have a Back Yard

My mama owns one-sixteenth of
the Turner acreage someplace
near Natchitoches, Louisiana, and

she won't sell her section and
all her fifteen cousins, whom
I've never met, are disgusted.

She figures if hard times
come again we could always
raise tomatoes or something.

You'll never starve, Mama says,
if you've got a piece of dirt
you can go home to.

But she's never told me
exactly where it is.

Bridges

Some people won't cross them.
Maybe they come from dry counties,
think you can't be high and dry
and safe from that death
that condenses in midfall.
True, it can be dangerous
climbing into the lap
of the bridge father.

Many bridges,
like the one at Pascagoula,
cross over drowned things.
Others are dead themselves,
flat and malignant.

The drawbridge down by Kemah
opened above the creek
at Mirabel's magenta whorehouse
where it hunkered on stilts
in wet, halfhearted indecency.

The one near Orange
was an absolute parabola.
"Oh, Lord," said my mama
halfway over, "I need
a Coca-Cola." Later I dreamed
I was crawling on my belly
up its left slope,
digging my nails into asphalt.
Then I went back to check
and so help me it *was* like that,
as steep as a bell-shaped curve.

And once in Houston I was
rushing to do something
I shouldn't be doing,
and I turned wrong
and went right
and started rising like
raw bread in streaks of heat
and kept going and going,
not steep but for always.

I could have come down in Fairbanks
or the Grant administration,
or met the lithographed Jesus
showing me his hands
from a cloud of petrol,
saying he wanted the Chevy and me
for higher purposes.
When I reached the farther shore

it was too late to sin
and I needed a Lone Star Dark.

Ten years later, this girl
in the bar at Arnaud's said,
"Friend, there is this bridge
back in Houston
that sent me over
and took me back
at the same damned time,
and when I sailed up on it
I thought my daddy had come for me."
"Yeah," I said,
and I named the rise exactly.
"You mean," she yelled,
clutching her third sherry,
"you mean it wasn't *me?*

But I had to tell her,
for better or worse,
when you're on your way up
in a cubicle of speed
with no preparation
it's partly you,
but mostly it's the bridges.

Southern Gothic

Poet in New York, revised. "Where you from?"
asks the woman in the Horn and Hardart
of the man with a tie wider than he is.
"Alabama," he answers. She's uncorked.

From her green beans she rises. "When,"
she yells in compassion, "will you SLIME

stop murdering Negroes?" and this frail man,
who only did damage to himself
with too much Scotch, hunkers down
in a city of razor wire, not thinking
to holler in return, "When will you YANKEES
stop mugging the Hasidim for their diamonds?"

You don't need this, Everette.
Come home, listen to your own folks
make idiots of themselves. And come back,
Eugene, from Rome, where the Communists
beat you up. Come home and let your own folks
work you over at Mardi Gras.

And go home, me,
where it's a mess, but a warmer, cheaper one.
Where nobody stares at my flat noises,
nobody stands on good geography
waiting, wide-white-eyed, for me to swig
a jar of moonshine and go South blind,
to kick a hound dog, whip out the whip.
They're sure I carry it, that lush disease
known as Gothic.

I should tell them,
That's man stuff, anyway. We womenfolk,
we only sat saying things. Like the woman
at the asylum, slamming down her hand
and shouting, "I will not play another card,
Ouida Keeton, until you tell me
what you did with the rest of your mother!"

Okay, so Miss Ouida, *she* took some action,
but usually we talk.
"They sewed
that tube to her BLADDER, and all the curl
fell out of her hair. Never did come back

'cept for one little patch."
                              "She had
a heart attack and laid there
three days next to the clothesline
with her face in the clematis
and the ANTS ate her."

                    Miss Mae Marie
asked the cop with the ice cream,
"You all find out 'bout them two men
that was hangin' in the TREE?"
Oh, not the Klan this time, just a suicide
with company.

                    The only person I know
who ever got whipped was my Uncle Jesse,
because, in 1910, he left off plowing
and slipped away to the schoolhouse.
His father tied him around a tree, beat him
ignorant with a buggy whip.
                              They do it to
kids up North, too. They just do it indoors.

LEO LUKE MARCELLO

The Behavior of Ants

> Ants Behead Queen.

The ants beheaded their queen.
She was riding their shoulders
when her regally big head stuck
in the new doorway.

None of her subjects noticed.
They enthroned her,
brought sugary platters.
No one could understand
why she'd lost
her appetite.

The *Post* reported the accident.
The zoo had to junk its colony
and start all over.

My kitchen is not such a zoo,
though a colony thrives.
Ants are dancing in my sink.
I have cleared my pantry
more than once, but
their samba continues.
My refrigerator is jammed
with exiled canisters.

I have sprayed poison, I confess,
until my throat turned red,
wiped thresholds with bleach
to repel the dotted lines
of invaders.

But they reappear near the faucet,
in the sink, in seams of windows.

I cannot make a cake.
I cannot let a baked chicken cool.

They approach my coffee cup.
I press them to quick deaths
beneath my fingers.

I sprinkle drops of lemon
on the windowsills,
lay lemon rinds
as casement guardians.

Nothing daunts these soldiers.
This morning in the war ruins,
I found them, wandering still
the formica desert, and on top
the acidic yellow dune,
a brave new creature,
a newly mutated species, I thought,
intended to survive all tactics,
waved a leg out of its head,
some strange new dancestep
against the war with humans.

But I was wrong.
The soldier was carrying the still
fighting remains of a comrade.
I pressed them both to death
into the lemony pulp.

I do not think ants think,
but afterwards, tempted to sniff
at this death hand, I wondered
how they felt crushed into
the bitter lemony pulp
and if it makes much difference

———
145

that the last fingers that press us
to death taste of the salt
that is human skin.

Finger Bowls

> Do you know what it means to miss
> New Orleans?
>
> —E. DeLang and L. Alter

We have placed our hands palms down
upon the freshly starched white tablecloth
at the end of such occasions.

It is not simply the fish-scented city we miss
but also the table-heavy course of life in it,
the linen or leather or plastic menus
folded all over town and taken from us,
in oyster bars, with cold foamy heads of beer
and the salty world of sea smells
and summer-drenched bodies,

and in elegant amber-lit dining rooms,
fingers clicking forks and rings,
a maître d' snapping busboys
to attention,

silver bowls with thin lemon slices
floating, occasional hibiscus
blossom on the silvery surface
of clear water,

ablutions at the end of feasts
of seafood appetizers and entrées,
meunière crusts, or their spicy fragrances
rinsed from our fingers,

then dabbed with a starched
white napkin,

every night
dozens and dozens
of these freshly
starched white
napkins.

Someone
in the back room
is very busy.

Les Fils

Quand 'Tit Jean est revenu d'Espagne en 66
à Noël et n'a pas été tué au Viêt-nam,
Papa a préparé un jambalaya et des fèves rouges
et a invité toute la ville à célébrer.

Pendant que le band jouait "Blueberry Hill"
et l'odeur de la bière Dixie et le gui
remplissaient l'air, 'Tit Jean m'a pris la taille
pour danser, m'a dit combien j'étais jolie et intelligente.
J'ai bu ses mots, comme tous les autres, je voulais
savoir tout sur l'Espagne, les courses de taureaux
et les jambes longues sous les jupons flamencos.

Dehors, les pétards jetaient des étincelles
et s'élançaient dans l'air, les feux d'artifices explosaient,
les chars, par-choc contre par-choc, klaxonnaient,
la levée illuminée par des feux de joies énormes,
l'un après l'autre, jusqu'à la Nouvelle-Orléans.

Après la messe de minuit, Mama
remplissait nos bols de gombo à l'andouille.
'Tit Jean revenait à la maison
par un chemin de campagne.
Son ami d'école filait à toute allure, soûl,
dans l'autre sens; il n'a pas vu 'Tit Jean.
Le grand shérif a annoncé la triste nouvelle.
Personne n'avait plus envie de gombo chaud,
ni de riz, ni de patates douces, ni de pralines.

Le jour après Noël, les amis sont venus.
Nous avons bu du café noir et avons veillé
le corps de 'Tit Jean toute la nuit.
Ernie Boy—qui apprenait à jouer à la pelote
avec 'Tit Jean—a pleuré, a vomi, et s'est endormi
parmi les autres petits au pied du cercueil.

Sons

When Junior came back from Spain in 66
at Christmas and didn't get killed in Vietnam,
Daddy cooked jambalaya and red beans
and invited the whole town to celebrate.

As the band played "Blueberry Hill"
and Dixie Beer and mistletoe hung in the air,
June whisked me to the dance floor,
said how pretty and smart I was.
I drank his words, like everyone else,
wanted to know all about Spain, bullfights,
and long legs under red flamenco skirts.

Outside, firecrackers sparked
and shot, cherry bombs exploded,
cars blew their horns, bumper to bumper,
the levee blazed with bonfires,
all the way to New Orleans.

After midnight Mass, Mama
filled our bowls with andouille gumbo.
June headed home on a country lane.
His high school friend whizzed
skunk drunk in the other direction,
he didn't see June coming.
The sheriff broke the news.
Nobody cared for hot gumbo,
dirty rice, candied yams, or pralines.

The day after Christmas, mourners came.
We drank black coffee and stayed up
with June's body through the night.
Ernie Boy—just learning to play pitch and catch
with June—cried, threw up, and finally fell asleep
among the other little ones at the foot of the coffin.

Ma sœur, Shirley, et moi nous sommes mises à genoux
à côté de 'Tit Jean, et nous avons prié et chuchoté
au sujet de l'odeur de la mort et nous nous sommes
demandées si tout le monde la sentait, mais n'osait pas le dire.

Le lendemain, les porteurs ont glissé
le cercueil dans la tombe, comme
on glisse une casserole de pain au four.
La pluie était froide et noyait
les rubans éclarlates sur les grandes
couronnes de roses rouges attachées au mur.

Ce printemps-là, Mama s'est adonnée à
la tristesse de la même ardeur qu'elle faisait
le chemin de la croix pendant le carême.
Elle a commencé à lire des livres
au sujet de la mort et de la souffrance,
à porter le noir, et elle a mis le chagrin
dans le boghei de bébé de son fils, a resserré
sa quilte à son cou et a poussé le boghei
hors de la chambre, à travers la cuisine,
et la cour de derrière, passant par les clos
de canne à sucre, à travers les savannes, jusqu'aux
eaux de la ciprière au milieu des lis oranges.

Puis, elle a arraché le boghei à la ciprière, l'a poussé vers
la maison, dans l'allée, dans la ruelle de la Grande Pointe,
le long du chemin du Fleuve, jusqu'à l'église dé St-Joseph.
Elle a poussé un soupir déchirant, la sueur perlant
sur son front ridé. Elle a monté les marches de l'église,
traînant le boghei derrière elle, est entrée par le portail
de chêne, s'est dirigée tout droit, s'est dressée
devant l'autel, sans s'agenouiller, a regardé Dieu
dans les yeux et Lui a crié "Maudit fils de putain!"

Les croyants se sont tus, elle s'est retournée
et a agité les bras terriblement,

My sister, Shirley, and I knelt beside it and prayed
and whispered about the smell of death
and wondered whether everybody smelled it
but dared not say.

The next day, the pallbearers slid
the coffin in the mausoleum,
the way you slide a pan of bread into an oven.
The rain was cold and damp
and drenched the scarlet ribbons
on the great sprays of red roses at the wall.

That spring, Mama devoted herself to sorrow,
the way she did the stations of the cross
during Lent. She started checking out books
on death and suffering, wore black,
and put sorrow in June's baby buggy, tucked his
quilt at its neck, and pushed the buggy
out of her bedroom, through the kitchen,
down the back steps, through cane fields,
and pastures, into swamp waters,
among wild orange irises.

She dredged the buggy from the swamp,
pushed it back to the house, down the driveway,
onto Grand Point Lane, to River Road,
to St. Joseph's Church. She heaved,
she sweated, the wrinkles in her face stood taut.
She pulled the buggy up the church steps,
to the thick oak portal, up the aisle, to the altar,
did not genuflect, stared God straight in the eye,
and said *"Maudit fils de putain!* . . . You son of a bitch!"

The congregation froze, she turned
and waved her arms wildly,

"Au diable avec tous de vous autres!"
Elle est descendue de l'autel,
frappant le boghei contre les bancs.
Elle s'est arrêtée devant *La Pietà*,
qui tenait la dépouille du Christ
dans ses bras; dans sa main suppliante,
un chapelet de cristal brisait
les rayons de lumière de la rosace.

"Toi, toi . . ." sa voix s'est cassée.
Elle s'est jetée au cou de la vierge,
a pleuré à gros sanglots, s'est écroulée,
comme si elle avait été touchée par une balle.
Papa s'est rué vers elle, l'a prise dans ses bras.
ª C'est pas grave, Mama. Viens, Mama,
allons rentrer à la maison."

Dix ans plus tard, les tumeurs du cancer
ont couvert le corps d'Ernie Boy, et
Mama s'est agitée de nouveau.
La mine effarée, elle a fouillé dans
les armoires, les hangars, et à travers les clos.
"Qu'est-ce que tu cherches?" Papa a demandé.
"Le maudit boghei de bébé!" elle a répondu.

"*Au diable avec tous de vous autres!* . . .
To hell with all of you!" She banged
the buggy down the altar steps,
down the aisle to the *Pietà*,
who held the dead Christ in her arms;
in her supplicating hand,
a crystal rosary fractured swords
of light from the rose window above.

"*Toi, toi* . . . you, you . . ." her voiced cracked.
She hurled her arms around the neck
of the sorrowful mother, sobbed and sobbed,
crumpled, as if suddenly shot.
Daddy ran to her, gathered her in his arms.
"It's OK, Mama. Let's go home, Mama."

Ten years later, melanoma tumors
covered Ernie Boy's body, and
Mama got restless again.
She got that wild look in her eyes
and searched closets, barns, and fields.
"What are you looking for?" asked Daddy.
"*Le maudit boghei de bébé!* . . .
That goddamned buggy!" she said.

Pink Geraniums

I remember the first time
I saw them, in December,
pink geraniums in her office window,
hot pink, the only color against
limestone, snow, and gray clouds.

The flowers grew all winter,
shameless of their opulent blooms,
their large, circular leaves,
the way they filled the window,
as if to say "Take me, take me,
I'm yours."

In those long stretches at 10 below,
I would take the short cut from the library,
through Denison, to Eisenhower,
time my treks with her office hours,
stop at her open door,
throw a "Hello, how goes?"
and bow like an old coot
from the Old West.

In my Ford pickup, I took her to Scheu's Cafe,
to chamber concerts, auctions in
Council Grove, Emporia, where
Flint Hills swell and dip, where
farmers and their wives unload
Bavarian crystal, Lunt silver, antique
Steinways, and head south.

In spring, when purple crocuses
pushed up from the snow, I took her
to my wheat farm, threw
a table cloth on the barn floor.
Her shivering under me, straw
mingled in her black hair, I kissed her
full on the lips, smelled her woman,
smelled tractor grease, the earth, and gave
her my mother's double row of diamonds.

Today, her long dead, and me 90
among white sheets in my hospital bed,
I see pink geraniums, hot pink, the only
color against limestone, snow, and clouds.

David Middleton

Hurricane

All summer off West Africa the sun
Poured heat upon the surface of the sea
While coming from the jungle humid winds
Wove up my torrid torso as it spun.
By August I was headed for the South
Following routes the slave ships used to take
Until my spiral bands, great arms of rain,
Would lash across the waste of salt and foam
So I, the dreaded reveler of the waves,
Whose dark locks raveled in the stratosphere,
Might dance my dance of death before the Keys
And in the upper Gulf when I broke clear.
Inside my giant eye huge walls of rain
Had trapped tired egrets, frigate-birds, and gulls
Flown to the clouded center of my heart
Where swept in the drenched winds swirling around
They drowned aloft, then sank in Breton Sound.
At last I wobbled and stalled along the coast
Where the mouthing Mississippi's lips of silt
Curled as I drove the fecund waters from his bed
Slicing the barrier isles as I would blow
Through twisted willow, oak, and indigo.
Once over land, now holding you in throes,
I spread my fatal waves through salted grass,
Flattened the cane so sweet and green and high,
Tore wires that brought you cooling and the light,
Smashed the chapel spire, plowed up the buried dead,
And left your babies hanging in the trees.
Then feeling weak and mortal from the rage
Of such great dissipation, I drifted east
Breaking up somewhere just north of Boston.
And though again in that strange way you gave
Thanks to your Father-God for being saved,
Accepting devastation as a part

Of that inscrutable act you call the Fall,
Your weathermen are wrong to take away
From half of me those female names so real
For I am Audrey, Betsy, and Camille,
So cast aside that patriarchal myth
And worship me whose pattern is the pith
Of all that is, the brutal womb of things,
Closed systems of the woven dynamos,
And know me as the one who comes and goes,
A fury in the matter I have riven,
Myself the only giver and the given.

The Family Tree

It always brought the fall to you off guard
This old pecan, its brown husks clustered hard,
While on the lawn's high grass leaves crisp and bent
Touched nuts and newborn moths with bitter scent.
More quickly then as if you'd been delayed,
You'd gather cabbage in the evening shade
And dig up late potatoes with your spade
In a garden that you planted near the end
From pride and need. Just there is where I sinned,
Though still a city boy who could not read
The seasons' book of hours and took no heed,
For once in bright July, in my Sunday suit
I climbed the pecan and plucked unready fruit
Smushing the pulp inside each pliant hull,
Eating rubbery nuts until so sick and full
I ran to you as you read your Bible verses
On the long front porch, your innocent curses
Holding me as you turned to where time weaves
Births and deaths and weddings in the leaves.
Then, distracting me from a stomach so torn
You traced the family tree till I was born

Once more. "Don't pick too soon" was all you said
As distant winds blew faintly overhead,
Yet only now, so far from summer calm,
The hard brown hulls held tight in my hard palm,
Can I suspect how soon you saw the end
To which all family trees and world-trees tend
In an old pecan, which, when the fall winds cry,
Shreds its dead cocoons against the sky.

The Patriarch

So near the unscreened porch's rotted edge
You stood alone, as always, unafraid.
Breathless, speechless, trembling on your cane
You stared ahead at nothing as the rain
Slashed across exhausted winter fields. But though
Your country sense and self-wrought classic mind
Told you one more stroke would be the end,
Like the yard's half-frozen asters you held on
Beyond the private self's demise, sustained
By public forms your life had realized.

Like you, the land was old, rugged bluffs
Whose rivers drained the wrinkled pinewood hills.
Blue clay, limestone, silt, the fossiled marl
Printed with whalebones, figs, and mastodons—
These weighed on sandy gravels of the Drift.
Even further down, an ancient basin lay,
Floor of the inland sea. Below it all,
Dead echoes of Jehovah's virgin word
Heard when you woke to taste in nightmare sweat
Its prehistoric salt, the Gulf's archaic bed.

Born between the Old South and the New,
You fought against the elegiac life.
But on an April evening when the wind drew

The bruised magnolias' fetid-fragrant scent
Over your slavemade desk, in Freeman's *Lee*
You'd feel it all again: the early victories,
Too easy, incomplete, the West ignored,
And then a smoky dusk through which there rode
As softly as the heartbeat's softest thud
The ghost of Stonewall slumping in his blood.

That was your native ground: for when you "saved
Democracy" in the greater world's Great War,
You met each German charge as though you held
Cold Harbor, your pounded doughboys not Yanks
But Hill's Third Corps at Petersburg, entrenched
Along the Marne. Later, as an ace, you saw
The blackened parishes of France, statues
Of the Virgin burning in No-Man's-Land
As in the Wilderness whose wounded spoke
In cindered limbs the long dead tongues of flame.

Back home you tried to live the civic life.
Yet even when as mayor you spoke each fall
Your ode on Flanders Field, below the drying
Courthouse oaks an orange-poppied fire
Spreading from Troy to Columbia, in your mind,
Troubled the busts of Jefferson and Lee.
At night you read *The Georgics* and you dreamed
Of that established land. But you were here,
A Trojan ghost plowing through Priam's dust,
The salted plots Aeneas left behind.

Warden, deacon, lector—Sundays you knelt
By the clear window. Outside, a rare bloodroot
And common roadside mallows stained the glass.
Here eighty years ago, stabled in the nave,
Union horses stamped in dung when brevet
Majors testing new repeaters and their nerve,
Pane by pane shot out The Kneeling Kings.

Shattered by that light, you read the lesson
Telling of a prince estranged from God by wealth
And foreign wives—poppies of Solomon!

Beyond the narthex-porch on which the sun
Still rose and set as it had always done,
You seemed a steward of the middle world.
Tomatoes, melons, beans, potatoes, corn
Raised by the posted roads of time and space—
These grew up to the house, familiar forms
To those raised eyes that found in the planted night
Appearances created and prepared,
Things in place, the flowering roots of light,
The constellations that were truly there.

That was your South, a many-layered tract
Of mind and soil, its tragic past made whole
By providential guilt and true defeat.
But with the last wild dogwoods rooted out
From cash-crop pine, you knew you'd lived too long,
A pastoral patriarch who winced
At sonic booms and heard B-52s
Droning over the Drift in lethal dreams
Of Eden as a paradise of power,
The massive Appomattox of the earth.

The house you built and died in long since sold,
Today across the acres kept so well
Lie only guts of disassembled cars
Disfiguring that domain. And yet between
The morning-glory vines and thistle-weeds
That hold the loam poured out from God's own palms
Uncultivated melons for a time
Will ripen in July, the cracked rinds
Opening up their sweetness to the fields,
The great red hearts riddled with darkened seed.

WILLIAM MILLS

Watch for the Fox

He lit it more for the light and
Movement it gave
Than against the cold.
He had felt the old fear
Skulking like a fox
Around a hen house,
Patient,
Time on its side,
People sleep.
But a jerk inside
(something his fathers
    had passed on)
Said to get up,
Go deeper in darkness
And get something to burn,
See himself again and
Watch for the fox.
Watching, he knew
The fire
Defines
The fox.

I Don't Even Recognize the Road

Louisiana air. Between water and fog.
It drowns me in the windlessness of my age.
In October there should be a bite,
A definition of what lies before me:
Brown pecan leaves, cut hay fields.

The thick weather instead reminds me
I have not gone where I intended to go.

I have arrived
Where I thought those who had looked
And thought hard before me
Knew what they were doing.

Here I am in their place.
I don't even recognize the road.

A Philosophical Evening in Louisiana

for Albert Waterson

In my neighbor's field
I have watched
Through the long afternoon
A white egret
Make his way from flight
To chained, slow death.

The old woman who owns the field
Owns the pond
Owns some mallards in the pond.

Each spring, audacious, cunning crows
Make their move
As the eggs are laid.
Precisely.
Other seasons their black flights
Seem random to us,
Their isolated remarks
Most notable in quiet winter skies.
Spring focuses their lives
And then the woman
Sets her traps
Atop long poles where the crows
Light to check things out.

She catches many cattle egrets
Who have no taste for mallard eggs,
But rather like to walk
Stately beside the cows
Looking for ticks.

Learning Not to Want

Where the traffic remains slow two hours past rush
we still sweat in our cars in late fall.
If I drove halfway around the world at this pace
I still wouldn't know what you mean to me.
My throat is hoarse from talking to myself about this.

It's all so public, this need of mine. It's become
common gossip like my grandmother grabbing her head
with both hands at the supper table in the nursing home
and shouting Be Quiet! And falling forward. And dying.
While at home I look with accuracy at death's clock.

I can't hit enough red lights to get the gist of this down
so I park along the side of the road by the canal
where a school bus of special education kids,
who look old enough to drive their own cars, wave to me.
Some of them, I can tell, like each other.

The rest is traffic, busy work, prescriptions for sedatives.
The rest is me with my keys locked in the car
and the ducks thinking this paper is bread.

Perhaps some day I'll thank you or by then learn
your language of resistance, and the special education kids
will swim in the canal naked and unsupervised, touching
each other with unskilled hands, and what I have
to feed the ducks will sustain them, and theirs. Perhaps not.

STELLA NESANOVICH

Fractioning

for my brother upon losing an eye

A light can go out in the heart.
—Richard Ford, *Rock Springs*

You will not see the trees this morning whirling
their green skirts. Blindness like a meteor
gouges a hole in your earth, this fragile flesh
we cling to. The spirit too has its secrets.
A light can go out in the heart.

No tears. We are all fractions of ourselves,
the children who played combat with iron men
and raced the dog across the yard, her collie's
ruff my horse's saddle.

Blood echoes in hollows where parents
and siblings rocked or read to us. Strips
of highway separate us—you with your head
swaddled like a mummy's.

Autumn at Midlife

Leave those dropped garments to sort another
time. Fallen shards of cloth, they will take their
form from gravity's whimsy, like you and I.
Here near the undraped window we can watch
the burnished leaves drop like tongues of flame
to settle and compost the earth to green again.
Here I meditate on the gifts of age:
anger no longer pent to parch the heart
and eyes of former lovers dimmed by yours.
I too have dropped my lustful masks, can wait

for you to draw toward the vermeil fire
of my love. Free of the giddy ploys of youth
we consummate a golden feast when love
recalesces, a Pentecost of autumn.

SUE OWEN

Bone Soup

Here's a soup to
fight the wicked chill.
Bones that give up
the flavor of their souls.
Bones that cannot remember
what body held them
together for a life.

Chicken, pig, or cow?
The only answer bubbles
its breath above the flame.
And identity doesn't
matter when the wind
still seeks more victims.

You can stir the bones
to rattle against
the pot, as if to say,
death is not peaceful here.
That is how the eulogy
thickens, sprinkled
with parsley and salt.

Taste is what you came for.
Hunger keeps gnawing
on your body as
long as time will last.

Take some of this bone
soup to fill your bowl.
Spoon it to your mouth.
The bones are passing on to
you, life to life.
That is the final sacrament.

My Name Is Snow

I want to report to you
that in my name, SUE
ANN OWEN, I have found
the word SNOW.
I can also spell out,
without much trouble,
the animals that
dare to live there, SWAN,
EWE, and that old SOW
though the SNOW
makes it quite cold for them.
This is not to mention
the NOSE that lives there in my cold name,
taking in and out for me,
I suppose, the necessary breath.
And that a SAW in there
saws when I sleep, and
there is NEWS, and the ONE
SUN that does not WANE.
And other words
that want me to USE them NOW,
like SEE and NO, and SANE.
And WE and AWE.
I haven't used them all up.
And for good reason I
don't mention
the ones I've rejected,
like NUN and NEON.
But one of my favorites I
OWN rhymes with SNOW, is WOE.
I also want to report that
without rearranging my letters,
my name backwards or
upside down means nothing.

The White Rabbit

You practice death
like this.
You wear your own ghost.
In the white snow,
you welcome your disguise.

You let the wind
blow through you
on its way to breaking twigs
for firewood.
You let the wind push
you as the snow leans
in fright against a house.

Winter wants to settle
your life in this cold.
A dispute it has
against your fur that fits,
against your heart's heat.

Already the earth
has given up its shape to
the falling snow.
You, too, should give up
the randomness of your paw
prints that makes
the hunter stop and wonder.

Already one bullet in his
gun belongs to your body.
Your dark eyes will learn
that when light
abandons them, the stew pot
had heard about you,
and luck was waiting for
your one loose foot.

GAIL J. PECK

Heaven

Ye shall be made whole, the Bible says,
so I picture Uncle John in need
of two shoes with both pant legs cuffed
instead of one pinned at the knee.

Terry, the foster child my grandparents
kept for a year, no longer on the floor
tugging braces up to his thighs,
pushing with his hands to stand.

My brother who was never able
to speak—words spewing
like water through a stone figure's mouth.

They're all there, I tell myself,
even the nonbelievers and suicides,
God realizing at that point
there were no more lessons to learn.

I'm not sure about the angels
shuffling between worlds,
with smooth faces, never aging.
I'd rather be like the Navajo woman
I once saw in Santa Fe, the wrinkles
creased like a fan along her face,

a face always open, watchful
except when she lay down
and the earth slept, having turned
on its side from the sun.

ALS

On diagnosis, Brenda's speech
was slightly slurred,
but now each word's a conjuring.
Soon even this will go,
along with the extremities.
One blink for "Yes,"
two for " No," until we're left to guess.
Shirley says when things get bad
she's having an affair
and telling Brenda, since she
can't tell a soul.
Brenda smiles a downward smile
and lifts it with her fingers.
For now, Brenda wants to see
her future grandchild,
take a trip to Europe,
drink, smoke, and eat
what goes down smoothly.
We've pledged two hours a week—
some of us prepared a little more
than others, having lost
a sister, friend, or child.
Does grief construct like muscle?
A tearing down then building up
so we can turn her easier
to face the walls she painted
Hunter green and hung with prints
of riders on horses with their front hooves
high above the hounds' heads,
the foxes nowhere to be seen.

Music

Grandmother was a ghost with red lipstick,
her chair chained to the bed.
She was singing, "I'm not Lisa,

my name is Julie." In the nursing home
alone again, as in those foster homes
where she once set fire to a monkey's tail
because, she said, he was mean and loved.

In atonement, she'd leave lines of crumbs
for ants—they work so hard—
and only after years of letting Tango in and out
did she lead him down the stairs to live outside
with other dogs, whimpering in the sun,
leaf shadows waving across his back.

I was to get the Magnavox
we shared with neighbors watching
"As the World Turns"—a large globe
filling the screen with distant countries,
the water contained, still. Instead,
I got the harmonica that made Tango twirl,
and I keep it with Pop's deck of cards.
Sometimes I take it out, running the cold metal
between my lips, though I can't play
and know nothing of music except the pressure
of one thing against another,
how hollowness makes sound.

WYATT PRUNTY

Learning the Bicycle

for Heather

The older children pedal past
Stable as little gyros, spinning hard
To supper, bath, and bed, until at last
We also quit, silent and tired
Beside the darkening yard where trees
Now shadow up instead of down.
Their predictable lengths can only tease
Her as, head lowered, she walks her bike alone
Somewhere between her wanting to ride
And her certainty she will always fall.

Tomorrow, though I will run behind,
Arms out to catch her, she'll tilt then balance wide
Of my reach, till distance makes her small,
Smaller, beyond the place I stop and know
That to teach her I had to follow
And when she learned I had to let her go.

A Note of Thanks

Wallet stolen, so we must end our stay.
Then, while checking out, the wallet reappears
With an unsigned note saying, "Please forgive me;
This is an illness I have fought for years,
And for which you've suffered innocently.
P. S. I hope you haven't phoned about the cards."
I wave the wallet so my wife will see.
Smiling, she hangs up, and smiling she regards
The broad array of others passing by,
Each now special and uniquely understood.
We go back to our unmade room and laugh,

Happily agreeing that the names for "good"
Are not quite adequate and that each combines
Superlatives we but rarely think.
For the next three nights we drink a better wine.
And every day we go back through to check
The shops, buying what before had cost too much,
As if now Christmas and birthdays were planned
Years in advance. We watch others and are touched
To see how their faces are a dead-panned
Generality, holding close
The wishes and desires by which we all are gripped.
All charities seem practical to us,
All waiters deserving of a bigger tip.
And, though we counter such an urge,
We start to think we'd like to meet the thief,
To shake the hand of self-reforming courage
That somehow censored a former disbelief.

Then we are home and leafing through the bills
Sent us from an unknown world of pleasure;
One of us likes cheap perfume; the other thrills
Over shoes, fedoras, expensive dinners;
There are massage parlors and videos,
Magazines, sunglasses, pharmaceuticals,
Long-distance calls, a host of curios,
Gallons of booze. . . . Only now we make our call.
But then, on hold, we go on sifting through
The mail till turning up a postcard view
Of our hotel. Flipping it and drawing blanks,
We read, "So much enjoyed my stay with you
I thought I ought to jot a note of thanks."

The Wild Horses

The horses imagined by a boy
Who cannot get himself to sleep
Are grazing so deep within a story
He cannot say what it means to keep
Such things inside and at a distance;
They are a silent governance
He feels but cannot name.
The horses change, and are the same.
They run miles farther than the meadows
In which he sees them run. They have no shadows,
Are unceasing, and they never die.
What he feels when watching them is like a cry
Heard somewhere else, and neither pain
Nor happiness in it, but sustained
Like a long note played in an empty room.
And that is how he waits for sleep, which soon
Takes him deeper than the fastest animal
As he tunnels clockwise in a fall,
The meadows rising through him, then gone
Somewhere above, until alone
He sees the horses turn in one long curve
That rounds them back where nothing moves,
And he knows that they were always blind,
Running from what they heard each time
The wind would shift, running away
Because they could not see their way.

To him, the horses are beautiful and sad;
They are a celebration made
Out of the way they end, begin again,
A morning's bright imperative sustained
Long after dark. They are a walling out
By looking in, what opens when he shuts
His eyes, the body's quiet allegory
By which it knows itself, a story
Told against the body that it cannot see.

The horses run because they're free
And incomplete, while poised somewhere between
The half-light in the hall and what he's seen
Inside, the boy wakes or sleeps, or turns against
His sleep, naming a larger self that rests
Invisibly, yet in sight of what it sees,
Rests without feeling, in the calculated ease
Of someone small, afraid, and fragile,
Alone and looking out, flexed but agile.

LISA RHOADES

Connections

Details accrete unevenly:
out of the window, shale embankments give way
to meadows of wildflowers, loosestrife mixed
with extravagant grasses. Disks of Widow's Lace
flash at the feet of bridges spanning the tracks. I expect rain.

You came up behind me in the music store and
touched my collarbone. I slipped the tape
into the tilted display, unable to answer the intimacy,
as when at Penn Station, a woman already seated
smiled at me, saying, "good, you're here now"
as if she had known me her whole life long,
although I had just entered the car.

Last night the Charles seemed a very small river.
We are inscribed by what we withhold
as easily as streetlights bridge the banks
and mingle in the wakes of passing boats.
We touch like young girls at the turn of the reel, hands
a fragile span above our partner's heads.

Does it matter that we decided sex
would have been the lesser of our infidelities? Instead of rain,
a low mist pulls like tatting from the inlets.
Perhaps the flowers aren't loosestrife, and the meadows
are only culverts. If I could tell the truth, what would I say?
The grinning conductor passed me my ticket like an allowance.

And no one seems ready to meet this train. At each station
someone stumbles out of the long embrace and runs,
bags smacking their upper thigh. While the people they leave
wave their hands the entire length of the train,
imagining behind each tinted square
the breathless outturned face they love.

Into Grace

White pelicans swell the religious sky
and shallow lakes of Baton Rouge.
We can only believe that we've been blessed:
coastal birds don't winter this far inland.
We give them a spot on the evening news
and a refuge on President's Point.
All winter we line the lakes in pride.

They squat on the ground or on half-submerged logs
like uncles on porches in late afternoon,
elbowing and arranging themselves
in a flutter of southern shirttails and doom.
Or preening, they snap their bills and click
like pocketbooks in chorus.

But clap your hands or call, and they break into grace
full flight, a gathering of wind. Your breath
draws in over their sheer size and wingspan
the delicate s of their bent necks,
their pouches flushing pink above their breasts.

Suddenly shy in their presence, you remember
a family reunion, you are watching
your cousin as she sugars the tea, stirs
the long spoon slowly, she's already sixteen and sexy,
proof your family can produce something wonderful—
that there is hope for you.

Carolyn Ricapito

The Man Who

We're all aware of a destination
like the man who
had his coffin made up early
a pine box
with a hinged door
the shelves were temporary
but, what isn't?
He filled it with glasses and bottles
it made a nice liquor cabinet
and
was an object for self-congratulation
every time he had a drink.
A man who knew
where he was going.

Up Till Now

Later, she saved for later, her lament:
"I was the only woman alcoholic in Paoli, Illinois."
At first, she only let you know
she was a journalist, beginning.
Now she finds herself
behind glasses, clipboard, pencil,
digital watch sirening.
Her body, a nervous dirigible,
scrapes uneasily table edges, chair backs.
Not yet likable, she carries too much
heavy stuff; to quit drinking,
do it all cold sober.
He was never even mentioned.
So in imagination grew large,
ogreish, threw plates against the wall

if he disliked the meal and gave her
a shiner the day before her sister's wedding,
told everyone, "The can opener is her best friend."
But in Paoli you had to keep up a front
and it was all so sad and destructive—
until now she lives in a tiny place
but hers.

Her House on the Wrong Side of Luck

Widowed by a yellow telegram,
she was my Aunt Opal.
I could picture Uncle Jim, falling,
trying to catch the bullet
already in his throat and out
while the First World War
continued to be fought in the distance.

I used to go and stay with her.
Her laugh sounded the stairwell,
curled high
in danger from the ceiling fan.
White shards fell on fusty carpet
where I sat cutting out paper dolls
and Totsie, irritable, old
dog, tousled mop,
wet, dark face visible under white bangs
gnawed Shirley Temple's leg
up to the dimpled knee.

SHERYL ST. GERMAIN

Going Home: New Orleans

Some slow evenings when the light hangs late and stubborn in the sky,
gives itself up to darkness slowly and deliberately, slow cloud after
 slow cloud,
slowness enters me like something familiar,
and it feels like going home.

It's all there in the disappearing light:
all the evenings of slow sky and slow loving, slow boats on sluggish
 bayous;
the thick-middled trees with the slow-sounding names—oak, mimosa,
 pecan, magnolia;
the slow tree sap that sticks in your hair when you lie with the trees;
and the maple syrup and pancakes and grits, the butter melting slowly
into and down the sides like sweat between breasts of sloe-eyed
 strippers;
and the slow-throated blues that floats over the city like fog;
and the weeping, the willows, the cut onions, the cayenne,
the slow-cooking beans with marrow-thick gravy;
and all the mint juleps drunk so slowly on all the slow southern
 porches,
the bourbon and sugar and mint going down warm and brown, syrup
 and slow;
and all the ice cubes melting in all the iced teas,
all the slow-faced people sitting in all the slowly rocking rockers;
and the crabs and the shrimp and crawfish, the hard shells
slowly and deliberately and lovingly removed, the delicate flesh
slowly sucked out of heads and legs and tails;
and the slow lips that eat and drink and love and speak that slow
 luxurious language,
savoring each word like a long-missed lover;
and the slow-moving nuns, the black habits dragging the swollen
 ground;
and the slow river that cradles it all, and the chicory coffee

that cuts through it all, slow-boiled and black as dirt;
and the slow dreams and the slow-healing wounds and the slow smoke
    of it all
slipping out, ballooning into the sky—slow, deliberate and magnificent.

Mother's Red Beans and Rice

The beans were tight and small as my young ass,
and I loved the sound they made when she poured them
into the pot. I could never resist plunging
both my hands in to feel the abundance of them,
the hardness and sureness of them.
In the morning, after she'd left them to soak
in the night, they would feel different—larger,
softer, the skins wrinkled like her stomach
from all the children.

She'd put them on to cook, adding to them
as the beans heated—ham bone with marrow
to make the gravy thick,
salt pork to make them meaty, smoky.

She'd scavenge around for whatever else we had,
always an onion or two, and I'd watch her
as she chopped them—I knew it was the onions
made her cry, but I also knew there was much
to cry about, so I was glad when she finished,
scraped the onion off the cutting board
and into the pot.

She always took so long cutting up the garlic,
mincing and mincing, and not really paying attention
until her eyes became dreamy and sloppy like they did
when she talked about the boy she almost married,
and inevitably she would cut a thumb or index finger,

and bits of garlic would turn pink from drops of blood,
and I would turn white—there was something horrible
about my mother's blood, it was too red, obscenely red,
so red it was almost
black. She'd bandage the finger,
gather all the garlic up,
throw it in the pot.

The beans would cook all day, filling the house
with their creamy onion pork smell, the sauce slowly
thickening, the beans slowly softening.

The beans were always good,
and when I make them now sadness falls over me
like a fleece, the sharp bean smells fill my lungs
like the smoke or blood of her—

I eat them like joy.

Hurricane Season

1

Those who have already been destroyed
recognize its signs: the sky
clouds like a glaucous eye,
the wind muscles over whatever
is weak. Waves swell, engorged
with too much of something.
A lashing, a swimming of tongues
through air. Birds disappear.
The smell of ocean in the wrong place,
of something diseased, lost fish.
The sky bellows, darkens, roars
like a drunk.

Those unacquainted with destruction
ask for wind speeds, amount of rainfall,
degree of movement. A plotting,
a computation of the destruction.

2

For some of us, all seasons are hurricane.
The winds gale up, working us like seed,
moving us like desire.

What lies beyond measurement
is all of beauty and terror.

To understand is to evacuate.

Govern Yrself Accordingly

i have dismissed
the minister
of emotional defenses,
distributed
confetti to all
the guards and given
faithful and ever vigilant
caution
several days off

the city
of me is well ready
to joyously receive and
rainbow celebrate
your unanticipated but
nonetheless profoundly appreciated
arrival into the intimacy
of our space

know that you are warmly
welcomed for howsoever long
you should choose to stay
here, you need no keys
no door is locked to you
every window is open

feel free

even death will not stop me from struggling

i will continue
as ashes & dust

my bronze flesh will join the soil
of free lands everywhere

& grow trees
be the mud within which rabbits burrow
be carpet of rain forest mountain walls
welcoming gorillas home

my bronze flesh
sacred ground
will become ancestor soil

and i will also be dry dust
refusing to cover despots
i'll clog the air filters
of tanks & invade the nostrils
of invaders

you hear that wind
that's my dying breath
laughing at those who thought
they'd seen the last of me

you see that baby eating soil
      dirt smeared around her cheeks
that worker dusting himself off
that couple of love embracing on
      picnic ground
that hopi sand painting
that amazonian striped with the chalk
      of white clay
you see me

i am sorry to disappoint you
but i do not die
i just move to another plane of existence
and become the fertilizer of the future

even when i'm gone
i will still be here
though death do us part

Where Are You

i seek you
with the tender urgency
of ocean searching
for sand to touch

my roaring waves slowly
climb ashore and, with
neither shame nor hesitancy,
break softly into foamy wisps
which insistently whisper
your name into the warm
ear of the wind

those are not stars
lighting the night
those are my intimate eyes

looking for you

Southern Women

Southern women won't shake your hand
when you meet them, my friend says,
they nod while their husbands

squeeze your palm and slap your shoulder.
We walk toward the mausoleum
toward bodies above ground, here land

covers seawater like algae.
I think of the women
I grew up with, kissed in greeting

in the vestibule of Sacred Heart.
Women in veils and without,
with rosaries and novenas,

sometimes with men, but
always with children, and always
when the congregation stands

before a dark space in the wall
of rose marble markers, and the Knights
have lifted their plumed hats

back on their smooth gray heads,
and Father has closed the book,
slid the colored ribbons in place, and

the gallant sword has been handed,
the flag folded in its tight triangle,
it is the women who turn first,

wives and daughters,
into the sun or into the rain,
their heels marring the soft black ground,

sometimes sinking, and whatever season,
they look into magnolia or oak
or wild azalea, something alive,

and the men, brothers, sons
lay down their frozen boutonnières
and follow.

M Is for the Many

I touched him more than is appropriate.
His mouse brown hair downy without Vitalis,
his taut finger around the beads,
an orange fleck of mercurochrome
upon the nail-edge where he'd pierced it
on the front holly. Will Jesus
tend his cuts now, Jesus
worn faceless in the pinch
of his praying hands? My sister

showed our mother a place
between his arm and right ribs,
inside the crook of his elbow
where he still felt warm.
She tells me his hands will cross
this way for the fifty years
of his coffin's airtight guarantee.
Long after our hair grays
at the temples and the soft
skin folds above the bones
of our hands, his lids
and mouth will be fixed
in the hard curve of
makeup around his jaw.

This is not sad,
as at the cemetery after the tomb
was blessed and the ushers
slid the long oak box in, the bus driver
asked to sing a song
for his dead friend's mother.
No one told him it was not proper.
He clasped his hands before him.
M is for the many
things she gives me, he began
to the clear sun and with him
was laughter and mouthing
of the words.

I'll Try to Tell You What I Know

Sometimes it's so hot the thistle bends
to the morning dew and the limbs of the trees
seem weighted like they won't hold up moss
anymore. The women sit and swell with
the backwash of old family pain and
won't leave the house to walk across
the neighbor's yard. One man takes up a shotgun
over the shit hosed from a pen of dogs.
One boy takes a fist of rings and slams the face
of a kid throwing shells at his car.
That shiny car is all the love his father
has to give. And his mother cooks
the best shrimp étouffée and every day
smokes three packs down to their mustard-colored ends.

One night the finest woman I ever
knew pulled a cocktail waitress by the hair
out of the backseat of her husband's new

Eldorado Cadillac and knocked her
down between the cars at the Queen Bee Lounge.
She drove the man slumped and snoring with his hand
in his pants home and not a word was said.
I'll try to tell you what I know
about people who love each other
and the fear of losing that cuts a path
as wide as a tropical storm through the marsh
and each year gets closer
to falling at the foot of your door.

The Last Swimmer on Galveston Beach

September, 1968

> During the siege of the Alamo, Travis
> removed the heavy ring from his finger,
> ran a string through it, and tied it around
> the neck of little Angelina Dickinson. "I
> won't have any more use for this, honey,"
> he said. "Keep it to remember me by."
>
> —Inscription attached to Colonel William
> Travis' cat's-eye ring, Alamo Museum,
> San Antonio, Texas

In the mountains
where the guns were,
the sheep graze far and lie cool
in the evening, dreaming the way
down to winter pastures.

Rising from the sand, he throws
a towel across his shoulders,
starts toward a place
where lights are coming on,
and voices, young and strange,
are gathering in the music
around a curving bar;
stops, turns back, and
and stands before the great Gulf space,
emptied now of dazzle,
filling with night breeze
and late summer dark.

The tide flashes white,
the only light,
and he is lost to me.
I watch the dark.

In our time,
he walked another beach,

a barrage mounting a cold surf,
running hard, and
in the still afterward
the wintry rasp
of dead boys against the sand.

In another time,
far up the long slow slope of Texas,
we sat with stereoscope and seashells
in a chiming afternoon:
Goliad remembered, the Alamo remembered,
the last Indian depredations remembered,
the Maine revenged,
the Kaiser down the hill,
we heard the waters of the world
rising in a great conch shell; and
in a vision saw bones of sailors
drowned in battles long ago
(in a Kodak picture
saw a young soldier face,
heard the bones of the AEF clack
in a maiden aunt's thinning breath).

We lived in big box houses
off the courthouse square,
and knew the loneliness
between great wars:
in the lapsing afternoon
before empire and despair,
the stories of the aunts
stirred the summer air—
a ceremony in the mind,
a manner adequate to event.

The music rises and the voices;
but they speak not to him, not to me,
vanish in the water and the wind.

I watch the dark, and
dream a flourish in his mind:
in the floating shadow of the earth,
he cups the oceans to his ear;
below the black far drifting seas
the lighted dead are gathering,
quietly talking, all at ease.

The Circus by the Cemetery

for Totti (died 1925)

The Comanches did not enter into the
spirit of civilization wholeheartedly.

—Ida Lasater Huckabay,
Ninety-four Years in Jack County (Texas)

That summer the circus appeared
in the West, beyond the cemetery,
in a pasture left frontier:
too stony to plow,
too scrubby to graze.

Where antediluvian horned frogs
had rasped across pin-keen burrs,
loose, sloven tents,
heaved up against the August sun,
flapping in the furnaced air,
confirmed every barnside prophecy
of a coming.

Dust bubbles rising in crusted ruts
boiling over Sunday shoes,
we moved by our pasture of the dead,
buried ourselves row on row
in the great canvas tomb;

and sweat stuck to sweat,
saw what we had come to see:
raucous pagan lions and spangled elephants,
blousy clowns and golden girls; and,
high above, four alabaster acrobats
swimming the close vaulted air.

But they missed the show,
who had bought it for us long ago.

Once this ground went west forever,
no visions yet for hire,
uncalendared and unclocked, a people
followed the great slow pasturing
of the buffalo;
danced their painted ponies
through the drifting buffalo,
circled their painted tents
toward God, buried their dead
deep in sun and moon:
bone dust powdered the reeling wind.

But they closed the show,
those graven names
fixed in an angel's dusty stare:
no visions unbought by Christ's blood,
they said; and by time
and work, and money, they said.

Yet in secret they had said,
a circus entertains the soul,
bought for us our summer afternoon
of beasts and men dreaming
what was before memory made the dream,
the circus in us all;
paid no more than they had to pay:
Comanche, Kiowa, Arapahoe,
and all the land of the buffalo.

———

DAVE SMITH

Out Whistling

Driving home I see the white heron on one leg
    yards out in the lake, like a woman
sun-glazed, dreaming next to a seaside rail.
    The lifted knee, down-delicate, holds
light in my mind so I drive around the block

to find its black eye again. The little globe
    orbits with me, hidden in my car,
all of us waiting, and traffic steadily rasps
    like breath over cancered tissue.
What did you want from me? No ripple comes as

one leg replaces another, the eye satin, hard
    with sun's burning. So much
of us flashes there I remember a wind's flare,
    an instant, your cigarette, a street
you crossed to find me when I was out whistling.

Wreckage at Lake Pontchartrain

Baton Rouge to New Orleans, hauling Route 10, workweek
    done, flying home with old tunes booming,
        road jolts, shaken by the bodies,
I come into the room of a long wood quiet as a parlor.

Wisps of moss like an elder's beard. I fly by two snug
    grandmothers in a Chrysler. Miles later
        I'm shamed by the glare of their
pouchy lipsticked fear, a melted look I see some dawns.

Whose is that law of the eyes? I turn loud 'Go Johnny go,'
    pop a beer, grin. Then I slow down to watch
        the insweeping lake, a carpet
stinky and black and giving under its crane stepping ashore.

The Egret Tree

Ghosts of our fathers flocking down at dusk,
    one by one you return and stand
  shouldering the dim western light. Limbs
    you stride, live oak chambers,
creak with hundreds of you, white-robed,
    abrupt as stars, or the flared

    windows of offices where clerks gird
for war, lawyers blue-eyed, in impeccable suits, who
    peck in their own endless documents.
        What do our people need?
    Dusk-wind sifts the tree moss like a beard
    in its fingers. Over the lake's

lull, past black roofs where some bend above meals,
    you descend as if elected to this day,
  summoned brother by brother down, the tree
    burning with starlight you bring.
  Night lowers black-winged as we pass car
    after car, penitents once, now

    townsmen only, bareheaded, surprised you are
among us, leaving cars, standing, making our chorus
    of oohs, ahs greet each new arrival.
       Some obligation or need
  spills us here, in peace jamming sidewalks,
    roads, freeway. Almost we feel

panic begin. Cries for help. A curse on your kind.
    Do you hear it? The cop's kick stand
  snaps, his cycle gouges dirt, blood's dark
    oil squirts but we won't move.
  We want what keeps you so calm. Little
    wonder water fills with *Amens*

    weaving the burst last red spatter of sun.
Sirens knife our breath. The stilled waters tremble

---

as we listen, trying to remember
how fabulous love is, and you,
brightness, holding a tree rooted in the mind's
hunger, the lake's ooze.

KATHERINE SONIAT

The Landing

Bay full of sunlight straight up
and down with minnows shining.
The ferry slip's great piles rot,

three on this side, three on that.
They embrace an emptiness
the osprey weaves through.

I like to see her big wings beat
as she settles to the piling nest,
then peers around,

perhaps sensing my shadow.
Osprey makes it look easy,
a mother who knows how to leave,

fly and go fish, then sprawl down
with her young again. I've tried
to learn the homing call,

their high, then low notes.
She'll whistle back.
I play we're whistling swans,

thinking it would be a good voice
to live by. The two chicks hear
my gawky song and hunker down,

preferring nothing to one more foolish
teakettle of a human.
I can't put my finger on it,

but look at her. Always she lights
at some point higher than her young,
and when she looks down,

there seems an abiding steadiness
to her head. Porpoises dip around
the ferry slip. My mother was one

who never got what she wanted,
burial at sea. She planned
a transmigration, setting aside

water and a dolphin smile
to return in. Some destinations
are always withheld. Always the future

we pinpoint our moves by.
I wanted another to go out looking with,
not for. Solitary, we glide about

in the abstract. But these chicks
are feathered bodies rising
out of the sticks. One spreads

wings like windblown paper ash.
She tries out her new weakness,
bouncing on pogo legs, then ducks,

some suddenness on the horizon.
From orange gobs of sundown
to the bloodied morning feedings,

I've watched this nest, wanting
to see life ascend for the first time—
a move so old, it's almost forgotten.

Country Signs

Another cloudy day on the Chesapeake.
June tractors plow, gulls dive in their wake.
I ride road swells like graves for the ocean's lost.

From chimneys vultures survey the soybean crop,
fields of tendrils root down,
trying for damp connection.

*

At noon, cows crowd
the best tree on the land, a shady spot
across the road from Craddock Schoolhouse,
boarded up, still the imposing matron it was
in 1902. I drive slowly to hear the dry oats click
like little dice-tailed cats. And I'm still picturing
cats as I cross Kitten Branch Road.

*

I take it as a country sign,
how the lady in a blue shawl
and the one in red
lean almost out of their lawn chairs
to talk low under the shade tree.
They share neighbors' secrets
over baskets of shallots,
priced and scrubbed to pearl.

*

It's meticulous work
weeding the floral rows
when all about the breeze's full
of heated pine and lilac—
powdery greens, the ultra-violets.
My mother smiled and called
it Rosy Future when she spread
that shade upon her lips. I purse mine
and lick, thinking back.

*

Road dogs and fat wild berries
know the SLOW . . . CHILDREN warned of on the sign.

This graveyard's filled with little ones,
their bones so many years past wishing.
How stiff the headstones look
near stalks of windy green,
a great sprinkling apparatus crawling
high above the corn.

*

On Old House Road a girl in tiger leotards
with buckets of day lilies
knocks at the back door,
hedge grown clear across the front,
windows boarded up far into summer.
Like anything with a past,
the whispering's almost sealed in.

*

Reasons must be good
for this village to be named Paramour,
a duplicity of sorts,
and the next farm is Rural Felicity.
I thought that's what I had
until one morning my friend shook her head
and peered at me, saying,
*you look like you need something
solid,* handing me an ironstone mug
to hold on to as I let myself
down into this journey—
spider onto something by a thread.

*

I swing into a cut-off, Chancetown Road.
It leads away, then returns to the thoroughfare—
like these gulls,
a mixed-up, plucking horde

after seed as they flap over Pickpenny Neck,
heading for minnows at sea.

*

Tough job, one man chopping
under the sun with a hoe.
No gulls pursue him with affectionate greed
or wheeling indifference. It's him
pulling his instrument down through the air
into the clotted field.
And again.

LINDON STALL

A Paradise of Gentle Readers

To name them was sufficient.
Not that his so doing meant,

At the time, say, it was tit
For tat. Noun-thing adequate

It wasn't. It would suffice,
Though, if only so he might,

If not know, then somehow be
Part of everything he'd seen

There. Sun high over the hot
Pink banks of hibiscus, palm

And oak sugared by the blood
Orange blooms of big African

Tulips, snuff-brown pelicans
Plunging to pluck up pigfish

And top minnow off the beach
Edge, cockle by cockle, king

Over a sea-sloughed scrabble
Of dead ghost crabs and Venus

Clams, god of black scallops
And the odd nubby jewel box,

He arked and jingled them up
Into a tongued jumble hummed

By the gulf tug, into things
To love, and, by saying, be.

Little Prelude

Our nail-scraped tribute absolutely done
The blackboard rose before me, mystical,

The mountain's cloudy Tables of the Law.
Yodhs dotted, taws fastidiously crossed.

The Logoi hung there, God-begotten trees
Of Jesse, moon-mulched omnipresent roots

That in His Own good time'll hum a world
Of *um* and *ibus*, syntax synced and sunned

To synapse, Miz Mills' chalky blossomer.
2:25. The rattly time. Hick. Dick. Dock.

At my back, blind as Polyphemus, clacked
The clockgod, Hunca Munca's run-down big

Boy, Heaven's tick-a-tack of sickles hot
To cock its hand up. 7th grade. Outside,

The new-cut aftercrop of grassdust, bits
Of red ant, onion, the odd rat's nest. I

Sulked, all fidgety and funked, the lord
Achilles, Shreveport's plump Apocalypse,

Athena's punk Kid Carnage lost to dreams
Of Xanthus hero-clogged by his own hand,

A holocaust of corpses. The board shone.
I saw the Sown Men rise, Word upon Word,

The incandescent building-bones of God's
Dominion. O fair seed-time had my soul.

God and All Angels

As every schoolboy knows, desire
Isn't the fretty blueballed fire

To diddle some cute little blond
Bit double-O'd à la mode de Bond

Nor is it this big bare-boned bob
Of Puck's-bait cognoscenti throb

And sob for. It's not objectless
No, it's just nothing'll finesse

A round word into its once-round
Root, re-ensemble sunburst sound

To something solid, something *is*
Won't faddle into fiddle-frizzed

Disaster or the gut-clucked scat
Some tubbo moons to. Only that's

The beauty of it, how each whole
Note's fat and flutter-flatted O

Each fa-flung echo plumps desire
To predication, spluttered fire.

DONALD E. STANFORD

Bayou

Give me not gain but loss,
The heart with weeping leached;
The oak tree is pleached
Excrescence drowned in moss.

Relinquish all that's fair!   ·
And seek for your delight
Far in the soul's dark night
The image pure and bare.

The Bee

No more through summer's haze I see,
In sunlight like a flash of spume,
The resolute and angry bee
Emerging from a flood of bloom.

The bee is quiet in her hive.
The earth is colorless and bare.
The veins of every leaf alive
Have stiffened in the altered air.

Elizabeth Thomas

Sunday

It comes, a green worm squatting
on top of the sugar bowl.
White-gloved I am everybody's beautiful
daughter; I am their stillness.
In the kitchen souls of chickens rise in steam
above the white enamel pot.
They mingle with sunlight
particles and boiled starch
and veils of curtains
the color of sugar.
The porch door propped open
the black iron a permanent weight
I consider as my grandfather teaches me
to draw eights. His hand curved around mine
we take the path past Italian Lake
cross back over the footbridge
then start again
returning as the iron continues to hold
back the door
drops like a black hole
right through the earth.

Whatever I touch becomes infinite.
My grandmother's scissors
add a definite weight in my hand
their clink in the cut-glass bowl
certain as memory
re-winds the elastic encircling
wax paper on top of our winter garden.
Traveling through Sunday afternoon
I become its absence:
In the silence of the pantry
shelves of salt and rice,
tins of flour whisper

to the dryness of my own soul.
Miles above spiral flypaper
distant as death.

A boy plays across the street
in the dark rooms
of his short life.
Will his soul return like mine?
Down in the basement
my father's photographs float
beneath his tongs.
He pushes at the blank paper like bits
of food on his plate
without appetite, without expectation.
A smudge appears, deepens
breathes its life till I am full-blown.
My father lifts me from the bath
and hangs me on a string to dry.

Visions of Doom at Canal Villere

Once a hurricane enters the mouth
of the Mississippi
it will be sucked upriver
into Lake Pontchartrain,
it will quadruple in strength,
tear itself free
and drag New Orleans back to the sea.

I'd always known I'd fulfill
my lifetime dream of regret.
Only those lucky souls
who reserved in advance suites
at the high-rise hotels
will be saved. Only those

touring the delta on the Delta Queen
will be safely swept
into the Gulf of Mexico.
They will have no regrets
having been photographed by law
at the dock, though lord only knows
who'll be left to identify
their pictures.

Never have I bought so much
beans and rice, candles and powdered milk.
Why not boxes of Belgian chocolates?
Why not French cigarettes
for the fat lady across the street
who lowers her basket
full of change from her balcony
when she sees me?
A little something from the store, Babe?

Today they're running specials
on visions of doom at the grocery.
Somebody ought to be informed
it's too late to plan ahead.

There's not enough time
to make that gumbo, not enough time
to make it last.
Believe me, I know punishment
when I see it dished out.

Let's suppose, though, I'd dedicated
my entire life to a single desire:
one poem—or one aria—one fiery,
self-consuming passionate saint.
Have you ever committed, despite loss,
beyond the footage of mistakes,
one selfless act?

I swore, having been a child myself,
I'd love my own children unconditionally.
Who says, with regret, there won't be
a second chance? Not true! Not true!
So I left behind those hand-blown, cobalt-
blue wine glasses, so I lost
a treasured earring last year,
so I gave up a child I never knew
in the shadow of danger and doubt.
It's too, too bad, too late.

I wish I could change my name to Forget
found today in St. Louis Cemetery
little city of the saved
where those forgotten children
linger above sea level
in tiny embroidered chapels
and ancient, airtight cottages.

David Tillinghast

You Stunning

These places where we walk
Hand in hand
These cemeteries where according to code
The generations are gathered together
For the afterlife you do not believe in
These gray places among the butterfly weed,
Touch-me-nots of our solemn sequestrations
Where I tell you I believe
In your brown eyes stark black hair
And long arms slender silver-ringed fingers,
You dramatic
In this pale blue light
Among birds of day
That roost uneasy at your step,
Spurts of flutter
In the crisp dead cedars,
You stunning
In the moonlight where you tell me
Among kneeling lambs, glinted angel wings
That we may someday discover
How to love
By learning from ghosts.

Snakebit

Deep night under the white moon,

A solitary man follows

His shadow west   out of

Lafitte Marsh   wading the black mud

To high ground and home,

The hunt over before

It began—nearly a day ago—

In a dazzling dawn

     the strike—a slap only
       a light slap at the knee

Of green wings whistling

Before the red sun.

Under a blue heaven of Orion and Cassiopeia

He wades the marsh,

Bewildered—a sliver of yellow

Fang clicks each step beneath

The skin of his monstrous

Right knee—what black moccasin

Rising silent as breath

From the sweet grass,

Head cocked, mouth white

As this spinning moon,

Mistook him   what

Went wrong in this pure

Paradise of serpents

He loves, has strode

Among, shared a thousand

Rich dawns with—

The hunter wanders the night,

The tilting marsh.

Wings whir afar, or from his memory.

The stars drift high and blue.

Orion at his back,

He walks among his serpents

Wondering when, how

He has betrayed them.

I Have Always Known

that I shall never be able to capture my father's integrity

Before I can wade but a few
Paces into the cut millet
Of this January field, a covey
Thunders from under my step
And I raise   and lower
My Winchester   and simply stand
And watch—the chill of the
Sopping morning dew stunning

My shins—the brown birds peel off
Into singles and twirl and spiral
Into the honeysuckle across
The ridge   and I will
Follow up and the morning
Will gently fail into day
And soon I will flex my
Shoulders inside my father's coat
And feel captured on my back the sun's
First warmth.   And at
The height of day a lone
Hawk will simply appear
And glide high over,
Head cocked, scouring at a glance
This rich field and flushing
A hill of gray doves out
Of the open, skittering them
Into the trees.

In the long shank of the afternoon
Six black crows will sweep in
From the east and sail
The course of the field and
Flutter into the tops of the bare
Hickories, every feather defined
Against the winter
Sky, clear as ice,   and one by one
The scattered sundown covey will begin
Their stark regrouping calls   here,
There, down by the pond,   and a fox
Will bark on a hill, an owl
Swoosh out of a shadow   and at
The end, the white sun will settle
With solemn dignity over the ridge
And the dark will close

And I shall walk back
Through the evening dew of
This simple place beneath
A rising white moon
Of imperishable integrity.

LISA VAN DER LINDEN

Live Oak

It grew there uttering joyous leaves of dark green,
And its look, rude, unbending, lusty, made me think of myself.

—Walt Whitman

Supine and sticky, lolling
under an oak one listless
summer morning, I held
a vigil. Looking beyond
the bulky wooden torso,
thick limbs like rafters
bolstering a dark and heavy ceiling,
I watched the sapling boughs
and gauzy sprays of green bounce
at the very edge of things.
But somewhere unrevealed to me,
between periphery and pith,
lichen and tangling growth concealed
the point that gives:
what I'd hoped to isolate—
where balance upsets, offshoots stretch,
where movement ends, begins.

Clusters of moss, like stoles
of dirt and grit, unravel
only themselves. For as I searched
the mess above, even with branches bare,
I couldn't see. Fingering the mound
of moss I'd pulled, half-wanting it back
in place awash in movement, sporadic

sways, like mine, I wondered
at the oak's elaborate structure,
whether its struggle
is process and working out kinks

or an attempt to undermine design:
prolific leaves, twigs resist roots,
flap, bend to topple
balance, swerving, swerving.

Equinox Breaking

I nearly swallowed my face
last night, yawning so wide.
My lawnchair pointed north
as constellations changed shape,
and I, befuddled as usual
under stars, unable to find
even the Big Dipper,
could only think about
the cool, plastic, curvy
planetarium chairs
that make you glad it's dark,
and how light erases the sky.

Then 6am, and purpling bruises
into day, dissolves the zodiac.
I squint and poke, survey
for evidence of change,
for layered, languid clouds
in every hue of white:
no rays strewn, no fragrant breeze,
just a generous sky swelling,
opening like mesh
Venus's flytraps,
clouds set to clamp shut
and swallow winter.

Science

Each week a new
papier-mâché planet.
Most popular of all

was Saturn, rings
and moons aglow,
then Jupiter,

its swollen birthmark
a hurricane
bigger than Betsy.

They inspired fierce
tether ball around
the sticker tree.

But when the man
who talked billions
and cajillions told us

the sun, someday,
will flare, expand,
and sort of swallow everything,

we already knew the Earth
was third in line.
After that, the planets roll

around the universe
like marbles, and
if that wasn't cool enough

to set us spinning,
Paul Vick's face
whitened and contorted,

and he convulsed hysterically.
He had to go home early.
He had no concept of time.

BERNICE LARSON WEBB

Breakfast Room

Standing before glass
panes facing away from the street,
we hold coffee cups and saucers,
balance demitasse spoons,
close enough, each to each,
that familiar scents of bodies, yours
and mine, tremble between.

Distancing, we peel
layers, exposing.

Like thin blade
violating ripe fruit
lifted from the silver
bowl on the sideboard,
we strip to false rind,
naked enough only to satisfy
pretended need, the half-lie,
mirroring each other's cool glance,
nonchalantly raised eyebrow.

Morning dialogue will not answer
hunger left from other times.
Do you remember nights of satin
sheets and cool wind pushing
through open windows, white
gauze curtains that brushed
against moist skin?

We probe, not
deep enough to kill
but far
enough for pain.
Wait for poised clock pendulum—
footfall—the
closing door.

Guilt

Sin is not a devil
with fire and smoke.
Sin is as ordinary as a picnic
in bright daylight.
What remains after
the bread crumbs are gone
is heavy, a weight
that will not lift.
Sin is a stone forever
at the bottom of the heart.

The woman went alone into the
barest room of her soul.
She sat and waited in the echoing
emptiness of the room
and the emptiness of the
corridor outside that led to
nothing. Forever sitting,
she waited. Sleep came
and she watched herself dream
of the figure who would ride in
to save her.

Nothing
entered the room.

Guilt is forever.
The once-sparkling brown eyes
of the woman
grow dim with her waiting.
The noose around her neck
tightens as she struggles to free herself.
She recalls the tire swing
and the cherry tree of her childhood
behind her father's house. She knows
the oak limb from which they will hang her
is sturdy.

GAIL WHITE

Old Woman and 25 Cats

My children call it unsanitary,
think 25 cats is too many,
want me to boot them out, want to have
me committed. My children are young
and don't know beans.
Wait till they're old and their skin
is washed but unironed taffeta, their veins
a railway map of Ireland. When you know
you're a bore to hear and a blight
to look at, feisty at best, curmudgeon
or shrew at worst, a duty to visit,
a hope that you die before your body
becomes just too much trouble, then,
my dears, you love what lets you
touch it.

Written on the Head of a Pin

> The word angel describes an office, not a nature.
>
> —Gregory the Great

The car breaks down with appalling
regularity. If I have bronchitis,
3 credit cards overdrawn & my lover
just left me & the white cat died,
it breaks down just the same. The
clutch goes, the linkages slip,
it blows a gasket, runs a piston
rod through the engine block.
Today it's the brakes, so I've done
the shopping on foot. And feeling
slightly suicidal, I look
around me for signs of hope.

Now is the time for a messenger.
Time for a drink and sitting
in the hammock, a good time for any
passing dragonfly, mockingbird, field mouse
or calico cat to say, "I am Gabriel.
I stand in the presence of God."

The Gypsy Woman Tells Your Fortune

You will make a journey over water.
How large a body of water
I cannot say.

You will marry once for love
and once for money
and whichever comes first,
you will wish it had been the other.

You will eat too much salt.
Doctors will begin telling you
to slow down.

Something you never heard of
will kill your parents.
You will not be ready
to take their place.

Your job will be less satisfactory
Than you thought it would be.
So will your children.

Your car will break down
when you can least afford it.

When all seems hopeless
you will meet a mysterious stranger.
It will be you.

DARA WIER

Winslow Homer's Blues

Though the book was not meant
for me, it's hard to resist

a man's good art,
like resisting a sweet

and secret kiss, stolen
from or meant for another.

I picked up the book
and looked at it cover to cover.

It's that way with books,
they have no single owner.

Crossing the pages, my eyes
stopped to linger

over the sheer depths
of a dimensionless dark water,

surfaces I hadn't anticipated,
fish, frog, lily, moth, exact,

particular, penetrating eyes
which looked right back,

two silver-black marks
I might take for a mosquito hawk,

plain red sun going down
over the anonymous horizon

like a cynic's Icarus.
He stood his apple pickers

at ease where golden air
fell through the meshes

of the leaves of shadows,
blackboard lessons in circles,

parallel lines and holy triangles,
and the deeper, fourth dimension,

lightened by a schoolmarm's apron,
checkered, her left arm thrown

behind her straight back, to hold
her right arm's elbow up.

He made his bodies as if someone
he loved would be living in them,

or someone living would like to be
near them to lean upon.

He showed how humans stand
and wait with their honest day's

work in their hands
for the ones they love to return

when where they've been
has been far off and treacherous.

He invited me in with candor,
humor, care and skill

into what invited him.
In love, longing or despair,

I've never walked his pliant beaches,
I've gone and walked elsewhere.

Though I would gladly have
been with him. His blues

matched mine in two ways.
He loved his blues

in likely and unlikely places
and made generous sense

of a composition's shape
by where he put them.

He made apples blue
and plums, canoes, and shoes

on reclining girls. He picked
blues for shutters and blues

for skirts and for Parliament,
blues for shirts and sails,

blues for fish, blue for the plough,
blues in waters and in clouds,

blues in eyes and for blue sky,
rising and falling, blues

for fresh air. I was grateful
to lose myself in Homer's blues.

I closed the book and put it back
with its blue spine unbroken.

Late Afternoon on a Good Lake

The water gives, it gets us
there, it gives to the footfall
while we catch our balance
to stand up in the boat
to begin to go where
the biggest fish fight
like nobody's business.
Skill and luck come
by different routes we go

by our own lights
and sun's light
leaves the water
to dazzle us so
that skill matters little
and luck is all around us
even when we miss
it moves to overtake us
it takes our gaudy lures
and tangles them in branches
high above our heads
or deep in water
bright because the lucky sun
stays with us a little longer
in the water the black oaks
drill their heights beyond
the other side and when
big fish mistake our lures
for food we bring them in
to the evening's light
which gives up to show off
the fishes' shapes and colors
because what we are
about to lose
puts its polished foot
before us and asks, *will you*
no longer love me, look
what I shape for you to see.
Two worlds without us
would not meet where we touch
look what we see when it is
evening and the ducks are
at rest we leave the fish
alone and turn to the ducks
who stand up for us and walk

on water while we chase them.
Look, somewhere luck is
shaking a cup of ice, I want
to drink that water.

Old-Fashioned

Next to my best friend I woke up,
    small and deep
in the unfamiliar middle

of her parents' late night quarrel
    over faithlessness,
terrible to find her in such danger.

I wanted her whom I pictured the picture
    of happy-go-lucky to sleep.
I didn't want to turn my face to see

what hers showed or if now she knew
    or had known all along or never.
Her mother was so young, beautiful,

dark-eyed and quick; their walls, thick-
    textured and creamy like cake frosting,
were fancy and rich with filigreed frames,

watercolors of Italian bridges
    and pastels of Parisian streets.
Her father's dog was a dangerous German shepherd,

her mother's car an exotic Buick Electra
    she could take for granted.
This was the modern world I'd been denied.

Her mother wanted to know who the other woman was;
    her father didn't care.
While I listened to their familiar voices

I pictured them a foot apart, no closer
    than my friend, fat, faceless, sleeping
next to me in her bed. I pictured the dark

house shrink around us like a muscle.
    Her parents' voices rose over the pale moon
globe we'd left lit in the room for our own

late night talk of travel beyond our planet
    and the men we knew would soon walk
on the moon above us. Her parents' voices

traveled through a new atmosphere,
    one from which no words escaped.
We were on our way to somewhere unknown together

when over something I don't remember
    we parted company.
Soon her father would be gone and later

she'd grow slim and pretty as her mother,
    her mother the same
as if she were a picture.

When I went back to visit we sat together
    on the side of the same bed,
working hard to say what we'd become.

Her mother called us through the house
    for supper. Glowing in the golden light
of too many candles, Italian bridges

and Parisian streets glowed in their beautiful faces.
    When to emphasize her thought
my friend touched me on my knee

I flinched. It made me think she'd forgiven
    everything I'd understood and not forgotten.

The Perils of Beauty

No doubt a fair face, a fine
high bosom, or some glorious
buttocks' miraculous curve
has crazed down to bedlam
many a beauty, foamed up her lips,
snarled her smile, and snapped her mind
as easily as a string bean breaks
in the fingers of the kind of woman
whose mind is always safe, who now sits
on her porch, rocking beside
a heaped bushel, snapping
her supper and tomorrow's canning.

That beauty's peril lies beyond
any skeptic's doubt, beyond
the conundrums of cool, inscrutable sages,
is historical, incontestable, in Shakespeare,
and in her memory now as she sits
snapping beans and thinking about Raybella Skillen
and how Raybella used to comb her long brown hair;

she'd stand on her front porch combing it out
and the sun would strike it and everyone knew
that every husband wanted to put his hand deep
into Raybella's long brown hair and Raybella knew
and would say things like "Keeping a neat head of hair
is the least you can do for your man," or "The Good Book says
a woman's hair is her crown and glory."

But one day Raybella wouldn't stop combing,
wouldn't go back to her kitchen, her green beans
and salt meat, and they boiled away and burnt
and ruined the pan, and at nine o'clock
she was still combing, and at ten o'clock
women were talking to her, but she just combed

and combed and stared at the sun,
and they had to go get her husband.

"Raybella's gone off the deep end,"
she remembered telling Mr. Skillen
as she snapped another bean now
and thought about how Jesus handled things,
handled them just about the same way she would.

Here in Louisiana

Here in Louisiana it is December now.
The eaves are free and even. The blank sky hangs here
and seems to wait. Late bananas
are beginning to turn, may even be
ready before the frost stops their sweetening.
Still, this weather winters a few leaves brown,
drives some birds still further south,
and forces roaches beneath the loose bark of live oaks
or deep into the fronds of palms, under old planks
or here and there in the warmer dark.

Today I realized I'd not seen one in weeks.
We live with them here, with their presumption
and prowls, casually, as casually
as we live with humidity and small craft warnings,
with our governors and hurricanes.
They don't distress us quite like they
distress others. And our complaints are resigned,
informal, furyless. Such small, quick acts of God
racing out over kitchen counters
are too fast for more concern—or swatters, usually.

Cracked, they stir more disgust than let alone
to romp over cake crumbs and clean plates:
being big as thumbs,

broken, such things spill their creamy thickness
like salves or clots or rancid lotions.
And unless ground to grease,
some brown fragment will twitch for a day or more
till others clean the carapace to pristine silence.

And so we usually leave them alone,
wait on winter to pretty our kitchens,
forget them till spring, till camellias return
and wisteria twines the fences of south Louisiana,
covers clotheslines, the backs of greenhouses and garages,
drifts over bayous and fields and out toward the Gulf,
the waves and spray, till on fragrant, rainless evenings
out on walks we hear a stirring, what seems at first a fine,
faint mist striking the scattered leaves.

AHMOS ZU-BOLTON II

The Poem

The poem refuses to come, it backdrops thru
subtime, loses itself in a crowd of tangents;
the poet sinks back within himself, composes a
history of the poet seeking a poem that refused
to come:

shadows knock at my door
old black spirits bidding me
                    come on out zu, come
                    play in the night
midnight gestures outside my window
dance ritual from the vision's eye
            & then the knock
                the voice
                    come on out zu, come
                    play w/the night . . .

The poet knows that he should write a poem
about the poet/writing about the poet
composing a history of the poet
seeking a poem that refused to come;
but instead he toys w/the innerself
just now wondering
if he is not the poem
that refused to come . . .

Ain't No Spring Chicken

one

I am as old as sin
quiet as it's kept

As ancient as an exorcism
from paradise

I used to swing by my feet,
make a dance out of trees catching me,
I used to stand on my hands and throw huge rocks
with the bow of my legs

I used to outrun daylight
home to a woman dressed in nightfall
older than the blues,
older than the grace of sitting years later
on the porch of a rockingchair poem

I used to turn my eyes insideout
and cure a headache,
in a time before color 3D TV
in a time before footprints on the moon
in a time before the wheel

two

Let me tell you
of a time long before Lucifer:
when the sky and the sea were the same,
when we could swim to the stars

I am slowdragging against the walls of a cave
combing the wind with my hair,
I wear a rainbow as my diaper
and a feather in my ear,
I am tapdancing majestic waves
surfing for the rocky ground
where the tribe waits

They throw chains out to fetch me,
pulling me in like old age
with open arms,

they bite and growl a song
which welcomes me

Even then there was more to the world
than meets the eye

ACKNOWLEDGMENTS

To the authors whose poems are represented in this anthology, I owe a debt of gratitude. Their interest, creativity, and cooperation during the journey that culminated in this book helped to free the long road to publication of many impediments. I also extend my broad thanks to publishers and periodicals who previously published poems selected for this volume. The following list identifies more particularly those individuals and entities who extended to me their permission to reprint:

"It'll Never Be Warm Again" and "Once in the Lacquered Afterform of the Dream" are reprinted by permission of Ralph Adamo. "It'll Never Be Warm Again" first appeared in *The End of the World*, Lost Road Publishers, 1979; "Once in the Lacquered Afterform of the Dream" first appeared in the *Quarterly* (1995); "Old Numbers," by Ralph Adamo, appears by permission of the author.

"Azaleas," "Pole Boats at Honey Island," and "On the Veranda We Drink Gin and Tonic" are reprinted by permission of Sandra Alcosser. "Azaleas" first appeared in the *American Poetry Review;* "Pole Boats at Honey Island" first appeared in *Columbia: A Magazine of Poetry and Prose;* and "On the Veranda" first appeared in the *New Yorker.*

"Suite du loup, no. je ne sais plus" and "Ouragan III," by Jean Arceneaux, appear by permission of Barry Ancelet.

"In the Marsh," by Jack B. Bedell, first appeared in *West Branch* (1993); "The Maker in the Sky," by Jack B. Bedell, first appeared in the *Laurel Review* (1991); and "Sleeping with the Net-Maker," by Jack B. Bedell, first appeared in the *Kentucky Poetry Review* (1990). All are reprinted by permission of the author.

"A Song," is reprinted by permission of John Biguenet and Ohio University Press from *Contemporary Writing from the Continents* (1981); "A Short History of Barbed Wire," by John Biguenet, first appeared in the *Georgia Review* (Summer, 1981) and is reprinted by permission of the author; and "Sestina," by John Biguenet, appears by permission of the author.

"Le Courir de Mardi Gras," by Darrell Bourque, first appeared in *Plainsongs* (1994) and is reprinted by permission of the author; "Holy Water," by Darrell Bourque, first appeared in *Louisiana Literature* (Fall, 1992) and is reprinted by permission of the author; and "The Grammar of Verbenas," by Darrell Bourque, appears by permission of the author.

"Oysters" is copyright © 1995 by Catharine Savage Brosman; "New Orleans: The Winter Hour" is copyright © 1993 by Catharine Savage Brosman; and "Tulips" is copyright © 1994 by Catharine Savage Brosman. All are reprinted by permission of the author and Louisiana State University Press from *Passages* (1996).

"Programming an Evening Away from Home," "Dance of the Wino in Lafayette Square," and "Homecoming," by Maxine Cassin, are reprinted by permission of the author. "Programming an Evening Away from Home" and "Dance of the Wino in Lafayette Square" appeared earlier in *The Other Side of Sleep* (1995), published by Portals Press; "Homecoming" first appeared in *Louisiana Literature* (Fall, 1990).

"On Watching a Young Man Play Tennis," "The Bride of Quietness," and "End of Summer," all copyright © 1975, 1979 by Kelly Cherry, first appeared in *Lovers and Agnostics* (1975), published by Red Clay Books, and are reprinted by permission of the author.

"first blue sky," "often after a public event," and "a geography of poets," all by Andrei Codrescu, appear by permission of the author.

"The Red Shoes," "Maison Blanche," and "Romance," all by Nicole Cooley, are reprinted by permission of the author and Louisiana State University Press from *Resurrection* (1996).

"Holy Family: Audubon Zoo, New Orleans" and "Soul Making" are reprinted from Peter Cooley: *The Astonished Hours* by permission of Carnegie Mellon University Press, copyright © 1991 by Peter Cooley; and "Bayou Autumn" is reprinted from Peter Cooley: *The Room Where Summer Ends* by permission of Carnegie Mellon University Press, copyright © 1979 by Peter Cooley.

"Violets," "Breathing Space," and "Where Things Go When They Leave," all by Lois Cucullu, appear by permission of the author.

"Family Gathering, 1959" from *The White Wave*, by Kate Daniels, copyright © 1984, is reprinted by permission of the University of Pittsburgh Press.

"What They Wrote on the Bathhouse Walls, Yen's Marina, Chinese Bayou, LA" and "Proposing to A Victoria," by Albert Belisle Davis, both appeared in *What They Wrote on the Bathhouse Walls* (1988), published by Blue Heron Press, and are reprinted by permission of the author; "Culs-de-sac," by Albert Belisle Davis, first appeared in *Sewanee Review* (Spring, 1987) and is reprinted by permission of the author.

"Not a Bad Place to Start" and "The Inheritance of Death in the Vesture of

Dance," both by Charles deGravelles, appear by permission of the author; "Birdsong: Analogues," by Charles deGravelles, first appeared in *Maple Leaf Rag*, 15th Anniversary Anthology (1994), and is reprinted by permission of the author and Portals Press of New Orleans.

"Le Charivari de Celestin Joseph Doucet" and "Le Feu-Follet," both copyright © 1995 by John Doucet, first appeared in *A Local Habitation and a Name*, published by Blue Heron Press. "Freshman with a Neuroanatomy Text," by John Doucet, appears by permission of the author.

"Children and a Great Aunt," "Eulogy for the Sears-Roebuck Catalog, 1993," and "Sac-à-lait," all by Clarisse Dugas, appear by permission of the author.

"Bathing Father," by Christine Dumaine, first appeared in the *Southwestern Review* (Spring, 1990) and is reprinted by permission of the author.

"River Witch," "Practicing," and "First Gift," all by Malaika Favorite, appeared in *Illuminated Manuscript* (1991) and are reprinted by permission of the author and New Orleans Poetry Journal Press; "River Witch" first appeared as "For Men Missing in the Mississippi" in *Visions Decade* (1989), published by Black Buzzard Press, and is reprinted by permission of the author.

"The Bog Sacrifice" and "Audubon at Oakley," both by John Finlay, appeared earlier in *Mind and Blood: The Collected Poems of John Finlay* (1992) and are reprinted by permission of Jean S. Finlay and by John Daniel and Company, Publishers.

"Thinking About Taniece, Buried in St. Augustine Churchyard, 1968," by Ken Fontenot, first appeared in *New Letters* (Summer, 1984) and is reprinted by permission of the author, *New Letters*, and the Curators of the University of Missouri-Kansas City; "N'Oncle Oréneus," copyright © 1988 by Ken Fontenot, first appeared in *Rhino* and is reprinted by permission of the author.

"Sky Music," by Elizabeth Gayle, first appeared in *Shenandoah* (Fall, 1989) and is reprinted by permission of the author; "The Derrick Man" and "Offshore Fog: Day Twelve" appear by permission of Elizabeth Gayle.

"New World in the Morning," copyright © 1985 by Norman German, first appeared in the *Worcester Review;* "Whitey Goes Long," copyright © 1991 by Norman German, first appeared in *Beloit Poetry Journal;* and "The Space Between the Stars," copyright © 1989 by Norman German, first appeared in the *Malahat Review*. All three poems by Norman German are reprinted by permission of the author.

"What It's Like to Travel Long Distance Alone on the Train" and "To a Friend's Wife," both by John Gery, are reprinted by permission of Story Line Press from *The Enemies of Leisure* (1994); "No Elegy for One Who Died Too Soon," by John Gery, appears by permission of the author.

"The Long and the Short of It," by Quo Vadis Gex-Breaux, first appeared in volume 27 of the *African-American Review* and is reprinted by permission of the author; "Jazz Rain," by Quo Vadis Gex-Breaux, appears by permission of the author.

"Plantation," copyright © 1988 by Elton Glaser, is reprinted from *Tropical Depressions* by Elton Glaser, by permission of University of Iowa Press; "Pilgrimage," by Elton Glaser, first appeared in *Louisiana Literature* (Spring, 1993) and is reprinted by permission of the author; and "Evening Services on North Rampart Street," by Elton Glaser, appears by permission of the author.

"The Weaning" by William Greenway, copyright © 1983 by the Modern Poetry Association, first appeared in *Poetry* (May, 1983) and is reprinted by permission of the author and by the Editor of *Poetry;* "Anniversary" by William Greenway, copyright © 1993 by the Modern Poetry Association, first appeared in *Poetry* (February, 1993) and is reprinted by permission of the author and by the Editor of *Poetry;* "Men as Trees, Walking," by William Greenway, first appeared in *Plainsong* (Winter, 1985) and is reprinted by permission of the author.

"Christmas," "Babe Stovall on a Bare Stage," and "Valentine" all by Lee Meitzen Grue, are reprinted by permission of the author. "Christmas" first appeared in *In the Sweet Balance of the Flesh* (1990), published by Plain View Press; "Babe Stovall on a Bare Stage" first appeared as "1963: Babe Stovall on a Bare Stage at the Quorum Club" in the *Xavier Review* (Autumn, 1992); and "Valentine" first appeared in *Louisiana Literature* (Spring, 1988).

"Horse Sense," "The Poet Hunts Doves with the Natchitoches Police," and "Driving to Work," by William Hathaway, appear by permission of the author.

"Fence," by Ava Leavell Haymon, first appeared in *Northwest Review* (1991); "The Holy Ghost Goes Out for Little League," by Ava Leavell Haymon, first appeared in *Shenandoah* (Spring, 1990); and "Sighting," by Ava Leavell Haymon, first appeared in the *Northwest Review* (1987). All three poems are reprinted by permission of the author.

"Epithalamium" and "A Romance," by Cynthia Hogue, appear by permission of the author.

"A Construction of Clouds," by Rodger Kamenetz, is reprinted by permission of the author and Dryad Press from *Nympholepsy* (1985); "Turtle Soup at Mandina's," by Rodger Kamenetz, appears by permission of the author.

"The Mermaid Story," by Julie Kane, first appeared in volume 15 of *Piedmont Literary Review* (1991); "Mardi Gras Parade," by Julie Kane, and "The Mermaid Story" appear here by permission of the author.

"Black English," "Sky," and "The Surfer," all by Richard Katrovas, first appeared in *The Book of Complaints* (1993), published by Carnegie Mellon University Press, and are reprinted by permission of the author.

Acknowledgments

"From the French Market" and "Thibodaux," both by Sybil Kein, first appeared in *An American South* (1996), published by Michigan State University Press, and are reprinted by permission of the author; "La Chaudrière Pélé La Grègue . . . ," by Sybil Kein, first appeared in *Louisiane* (1982) and is reprinted by permission of the author; and "The Pot Calls the Coffeepot . . . ," by Sybil Kein, appears by permission of the author.

"Ode to Languor" and "The Potato Mash," by David Kirby, appear by permission of the author.

"Lingo," "Mud," and "Double Exposure," by Yusef Komunyakaa, appear by permission of the author.

"Baton Rouge" and "Migration," both by Pinkie Gordon Lane, are reprinted by permission of the author and Louisiana State University Press from *Girl at the Window* (1991); "I Never Scream," by Pinkie Gordon Lane, appears by permission of the author.

"Why I Have a Back Yard" and "Bridges," both by Martha McFerren, are reprinted by permission of the author and Wampeter Press from *Get Me Out of Here!* (1984); "Southern Gothic," by Martha McFerren, is reprinted by permission of the author and Helicon Nine Editions from *Women in Cars* (1992).

"The Behavior of Ants," by Leo Luke Marcello, appears in *Nothing Grows in One Place Forever* (1998) and is reprinted by permission of the author and Time Being Books; "Finger Bowls," by Leo Luke Marcello, appears by permission of the author.

"Les Fils," by Beverly Matherne, is reprinted by permission of Cross-Cultural Communications from *La Grande Pointe* (1995); "Sons," by Beverly Matherne, was originally published by New Rivers Press in *Two Worlds Walking: Short Stories, Essays, and Poetry by Writers with Mixed Heritages* (1994) and is reprinted by permission of the author; and "Pink Geraniums," by Beverly Matherne, appears by permission of the author.

"Hurricane," by David Middleton, appears by permission of the author; "The Family Tree," by David Middleton, first appeared in the *Sewanee Review* (Winter, 1990) and is reprinted by permission of the author; and "The Patriarch," by David Middleton, is reprinted by permission of the author and Louisiana State University Press from *The Burning Fields* (1991).

"Watch for the Fox," "I Don't Even Recognize the Road," and "A Philosophical Evening in Louisiana," all by William Mills, appear by permission of the author.

"Learning Not to Want," by Kay Murphy, appears by permission of the author.

"Fractioning," by Stella Nesanovich, first appeared as "Fractioning—For My

Acknowledgments

Brother Upon Losing an Eye" in *Christianity and Literature* and is reprinted by permission of the author; "Autumn at Midlife," by Stella Nesanovich, first appeared in *Louisiana English Journal* (1996) and is reprinted by permission of the author.

"Bone Soup," "My Name Is Snow," and "The White Rabbit," all by Sue Owen, are reprinted by permission of the author and Ohio State University Press from *The Book of Winter* (1988).

"Heaven," "ALS," and "Music," all by Gail Peck, are reprinted by permission of the author and the North Carolina Writers' Network from *New River.*

"Learning the Bicycle," "A Note of Thanks," and "The Wild Horses," all by Wyatt Prunty, are reprinted by permission of the author and the Johns Hopkins University Press. "Learning the Bicycle" and "The Wild Horses" first appeared in *Balance as Belief* (1989), and "A Note of Thanks" was first published in *The Run of the House* (1993).

"Connections," by Lisa Rhoades, first appeared in *Chelsea* (Spring, 1995) and is reprinted by permission of the author; "Into Grace," by Lisa Rhoades, appears by permission of the author.

"The Man Who," is reprinted by permission of Carolyn Ricapito and the Private Press of Fredric Brewer from *Destinations* (1977); "Up Till Now," by Carolyn Ricapito, appears by permission of the author; and "Her House on the Wrong Side of Luck," copyright © 1991 by Carolyn Ricapito, was first published by the Chester H. Jones Foundation and is reprinted by permission of the author.

"Going Home: New Orleans," by Sheryl St. Germain, first appeared in *Louisiana Literature* (Fall, 1988) and is reprinted by permission of the author; "Mother's Red Beans and Rice," by Sheryl St. Germain, first appeared in *TriQuarterly* (Spring-Summer, 1991) and is reprinted by permission of the author; and "Hurricane Season," by Sheryl St. Germain, is reprinted by permission of the author and Slough Press from *Making Bread at Midnight* (1994).

"Govern Yrself Accordingly," "even death will not stop me from struggling," and "Where Are You," by Kalamu ya Salaam, are reprinted by permission of the author.

"Southern Women," by Martha Serpas, first appeared in *Tar River Poetry* (Spring, 1989) and is reprinted by permission of the author; "M Is for the Many," by Martha Serpas, first appeared in *Columbia* (1990) and is reprinted by permission of the author; and "I'll Try to Tell You What I Know," by Martha Serpas, appears by permission of the author.

"The Last Swimmer on Galveston Beach" and "The Circus by the Cemetery," copyright © 1995 by Lewis P. Simpson, are reprinted by permission of the author from his chapbook *The Circus by the Cemetery.*

"Out Whistling," "Wreckage at Lake Pontchartrain," and "The Egret Tree," by

Dave Smith, are reprinted by permission of the author and Bloodaxe Books from *Night Pleasures: Selected and New Poems* (1992). "Wreckage at Lake Pontchartrain" originally appeared in the *New Yorker* (1991).

"The Landing," by Katherine Soniat, first appeared in *Manoa* (Summer, 1996) and is reprinted by permission of the author; and "Country Signs," by Katherine Soniat, appears by permission of the author.

"A Paradise of Gentle Readers," "Little Prelude," and "God and All Angels," by Lindon Stall, appear by permission of the author.

"Bayou," copyright © 1955, 1983 by Donald E. Stanford, appeared earlier in *The Traveler* (Cummington Press, 1955) and *The Cartesian Principle* (Barth Press, 1984) and is reprinted by permission of the author; and "The Bee," by Donald E. Stanford, appears by permission of the author.

"Sunday," by Elizabeth Thomas, appears by permission of the author; "Visions of Doom at Canal Villere," by Elizabeth Thomas, first appeared in the *Maple Leaf Rag*, 15th Anniversary Anthology (1994), and is reprinted by permission of the author and Portals Press of New Orleans.

"I Have Always Known," by David Tillinghast, first appeared in the *Georgia Review* (Fall, 1991) and is reprinted by permission of the author; "Snakebit," copyright © 1989 by David Tillinghast, first appeared in *Charleston Magazine* and is reprinted by permission of the author; "You Stunning," by David Tillinghast, is reprinted by permission of the author and the University of South Carolina Press from *From the Green Horseshoe: Poems by James Dickey's Students* (1989).

"Live Oak," "Equinox Breaking," and "Science," by Lisa van der Linden, appear by permission of the author.

"Breakfast Room" and "Guilt," by Bernice Larson Webb, appeared earlier in *Mating Dance* (1996) and are reprinted by permission of the author.

"Old Woman and 25 Cats," by Gail White, first appeared in *Midwest Quarterly* (1992) and is reprinted by permission of the author; "Written on the Head of a Pin," by Gail White, first appeared in *South Coast Poetry Journal* (1990) and is reprinted by permission of the author; and "The Gypsy Woman Tells Your Fortune," by Gail White, first appeared in *Descant* (Spring, 1982) and is reprinted by permission of the author.

"Winslow Homer's Blues" is reprinted from Dara Wier: *Blue for the Plough* by permission of Carnegie Mellon University Press, copyright © 1992 by Dara Wier; "Late Afternoon on a Good Lake" is reprinted from Dara Wier: *All You Have in Common* by permission of Carnegie Mellon University Press, copyright © 1984 by Dara Wier; and "Old-Fashioned" is reprinted from Dara Wier: *The Book of Knowledge* by permission of Carnegie Mellon University Press, copyright © 1988 by Dara Wier.

Acknowledgments

"The Perils of Beauty" and "Here in Louisiana" are reprinted from *In Primary Light* by John Wood, by permission of the University of Iowa Press, copyright © 1994 by John Wood.

"The Poem," by Ahmos Zu-Bolton II, first appeared in *Poems by Blacks* (1975), edited by Pinkie Gordon Lane and published by South and West Press, and is reprinted by permission of the author; "Ain't No Spring Chicken," by Ahmos Zu-Bolton II, appears by permission of the author.

CONTRIBUTORS

RALPH ADAMO teaches creative writing at Loyola University of New Orleans, where he is editor of *New Orleans Review*. His books of poetry include *Sadness at the Private University, The End of the World*, and *Hanoi Rose*. He coedited, and wrote the introduction to, Everette Maddox's posthumously published book *American Waste*.

SANDRA ALCOSSER has received two National Endowment for the Arts fellowships, a Breadloaf fellowship, and a Pushcart Prize for her work in poetry. Her first book of poems, *A Fish to Feed All Hunger*, was named the Associated Writing Programs Award Series Winner in poetry. Her third collection, *Except by Nature*, was selected for the National Poetry Series. She teaches writing at San Diego State University but otherwise makes her home in Florence, Montana.

JEAN ARCENEAUX is the pseudonym of Barry Ancelet, whose poetry has appeared in numerous anthologies and journals devoted to French literature. In addition, he has given readings at the Centre Pompidou in Paris and the Festival Internationale du Livre in Quebec, Ottawa, and Montreal.

JACK B. BEDELL teaches at Southeastern Louisiana University in Hammond and serves as poetry editor for *Louisiana Literature*. His poems and essays have appeared in *Kentucky Poetry Review, Laurel Review, Southern Humanities Review*, and other journals. His chapbook *Sleeping with the Net-Maker* won the 1994 Devil's Millhopper book competition, and his full-length collection *At the Bonehouse* has won the 1998 Breakthrough Award in poetry.

JOHN BIGUENET has published several books, including *Foreign Fictions, The Craft of Translation,* and *Theories of Translation.* His work has also appeared in the *Greensboro Review,* the *Georgia Review,* the *North American Review,* and other journals. He has served five terms on the literature panel of the National Endowment for the Arts and is past president of the American Literary Translators Association. He is professor of English at Loyola University in New Orleans.

DARRELL BOURQUE teaches literature and creative writing and directs the Interdisciplinary Humanities Program at the University of Southwestern Louisiana in Lafayette. He is a past president of the National Association for Humanities Education. His *Plainsongs of the Marais Bouleur* was published in 1993 and *The Doors Between Us* in 1998.

CATHARINE SAVAGE BROSMAN has published several collections of poetry: *Abiding Winter, Watering, Journeying from Canyon de Chelly,* and *Passages.* She is also the author of *"The Shimmering Maya" and Other Essays.* She is professor emerita in French at Tulane University in New Orleans and served as De Velling and Willis Visiting Professor at the University of Sheffield in England.

MAXINE CASSIN is the author of three published collections of poetry: *Nine by Three, A Touch of Recognition,* and *Turnip's Blood.* In addition to writing poems, she also serves as editor and publisher of the New Orleans Poetry Journal Press.

KELLY CHERRY, professor of English at the University of Wisconsin at Madison, has published numerous books in various genres, including *God's Loud Hand* (poems), *The Exiled Heart* (autobiography), *My Life and Dr. Joyce Brothers* (stories), and *Augusta Played* (novel). Her most recent collection of poems is *Death and Transfiguration.* She received the first James G. Hanes Poetry Prize of the Fellowship of Southern Writers. Her fiction is found in the prize anthologies *Best American Short Stories* and *New Stories from the South.*

ANDREI CODRESCU is a poetry writer and weekly commentator on National Public Radio. His recent works include *Belligerence, "The Muse Is*

Always Half-Dressed in New Orleans" and Other Essays, and *Road Scholar: Coast to Coast Late in the Century* (the book and the film). He edits and publishes *Exquisite Corpse,* a bimonthly journal of books and ideas, and teaches English at Louisiana State University in Baton Rouge.

NICOLE COOLEY has published fiction and poetry in the *Nation, Poetry Field,* the *Iowa Review, Ploughshares,* and other journals. In 1994 she received a "Discovery" Award, sponsored by the *Nation,* and in 1995 the Walt Whitman Award from the Academy of American Poets for the book *Resurrection.*

PETER COOLEY, who has lived in New Orleans since 1975, has published five books of poems, the most recent of which are *The Van Gogh Notebook* and *The Astonished Hours.* His work also appears in *The Morrow Anthology of Younger American Poets* and in *New American Poets of the '90's.* He is a frequent presenter-reader at the Deep South Writers Conference.

LOIS CUCULLU has served as a Fulbright scholar and visiting lecturer at Seoul National University and as a fellow in residence at the Virginia Center for the Creative Arts. Her poems have appeared in *Hawaii Pacific Review, Colorado Review, Louisiana Literature,* and *Poet Lore.*

KATE DANIELS has published three collections of her work: *The White Wave, The Niobe Poems,* and *Four Testimonies.* She also edited *Out of Silence: Selected Poems of Muriel Rukeyser.* She lives and writes in Nashville, though she yearns to return to south Louisiana.

ALBERT BELISLE DAVIS has published a collection of poetry, *What They Wrote on the Bathhouse Walls,* and two novels, *Leechtime* and *Marquis at Bay.* His story "The Mississippiman's Son" appeared in *Something in Common: Contemporary Louisiana Stories.* He is a recent recipient of the Louisiana Division of the Arts Literary Fellowship.

CHARLES DEGRAVELLES is a founder of the New Playwrights' Theater and former co-host of "Writers' Voices" on WRKF, Baton Rouge. He has served on the literature panel of the Louisiana Division of the Arts and as coeditor of the New Orleans Poetry Journal Press. His full-length collection of poems is *The Well Governed Son*.

JOHN DOUCET is a National Institutes of Health fellow in molecular genetics at Louisiana State University Medical Center in New Orleans, where he studies inherited diseases in populations of Acadian ancestry. He is the author of three "Cajun-culture" plays and a book of poems titled *A Local Habitation and a Name: Poems from the Lafourche Country*.

CLARISSE DUGAS is a native of the Acadiana area whose poems have been published in several anthologies and numerous reviews, including *Acadie Tropicale, North of Wakulla, Revue de Louisiane, Blue Unicorn*, and *American Institute of Discussion*.

CHRISTINE DUMAINE has won an Academy of American Poets award, the Deep South Writers Conference Competition, and the Billy Murray Denny Poetry Competition. Her poems have appeared in the *Mississippi Valley Review*, the *Xavier Review*, and *Louisiana Literature*.

MALAIKA FAVORITE, a visual artist as well as a poet, is the author of *Illuminated Manuscript*, a collection of her poems and prints. Her writing has appeared in *Visions International, Gallery: Women's Art, Studio: A Journal of Christian Writing, SAGE: A Scholarly Journal on Black Women*, and *Art Papers*.

JOHN FINLAY is the author of *A Prayer to the Father, Flaubert in Egypt*, and the posthumously published *Mind and Blood: The Collected Poems of John Finlay*, edited by poet David Middleton.

KEN FONTENOT is a translator of German poetry and fiction as well as a poet. His works have been collected in *After the Days of Miami* and *All My Animals and Stars*, which won the Austin Book Award. He credits poet William Hathaway as having significantly influenced his poetry.

ELIZABETH GAYLE grew up in Gueydan, a farm town in southwest Louisiana. She has had jobs ranging from roustabout on an offshore oil rig to poetry editor of the *Greensboro Review*. Her poems have appeared in *Shenandoah, Louisiana Literature,* and *Georgia State University Review.*

NORMAN GERMAN has published two Louisiana novels, *The Liberation of Bonner Child* and *No Other World,* the latter of which won first prize in the 1991 Deep South Writers Conference competition. His short story "The Arrow That Never Came Down" was featured in the tenth anniversary issue of *Louisiana Life* as its first piece of fiction.

JOHN GERY is the author of two books of poems, *Charlemagne: A Song of Gestures* and *The Enemies of Leisure,* as well as two chapbooks. He has received an Academy of American Poets prize, two Deep South Writers Conference awards, a Plumbers Ink Poetry Award, and a fellowship in creative writing from the National Endowment for the Arts.

QUO VADIS GEX-BREAUX has published poems in numerous journals including *Nkombo, African American Review,* and *Black River Journal.* Her works appear in the anthology *Word Up,* and in Spanish translation in *Quimera* of Barcelona. She also contributed to *Life Notes,* a collection of personal writing by contemporary Black women.

ELTON GLASER has published three collections of his poems: *Relics, Tropical Depressions,* and *Color Photographs of the Ruins.* He has been awarded two fellowships from the National Endowment for the Arts and three from the Ohio Arts Council, as well as the Iowa Poetry Prize and the Randall Jarrell Poetry Prize. His poem "Undead White European Male" was included in *The Best American Poetry 1995.*

WILLIAM GREENWAY is professor of English at Youngstown State University in Ohio. He has published three collections of poetry: *Pressure Under Grace, Where We've Been,* and *Rain in Most Places.* His work has appeared in *Poetry, American Poetry Review,* the *Southern Review,* and *Prairie Schooner.*

LEE MEITZEN GRUE is the former director of the New Orleans Poetry Forum and the First Backyard Poetry Theater. Her work has won the Deep

South Writers Conference competition, Roberts Writing Awards, and a PEN Syndicated Fiction Award. She has also held a fellowship in fiction from the National Endowment for the Arts.

WILLIAM HATHAWAY is "a recovering Louisianian" who taught at Louisiana State University in Baton Rouge for thirteen years before moving out of state. He has published several books of poems, the most recent being *Looking into the Heart of Light*.

AVA LEAVELL HAYMON has published in various journals and produced five chapbooks: *A Name Gift for Every Child, Kitchen Heat, Built in Fear of Heat, Staving off Rapture*, and *Why the Groundhog Fears Her Shadow*. Her poem "Jan 6: American Calendar" was recorded by Slow River Sounds. The theater company Playmakers in Baton Rouge produces her plays for audiences of children all over south Louisiana.

CYNTHIA HOGUE teaches in the creative writing program at the University of New Orleans, where she also directs the Women's Center. Her poems have appeared in *Puerto del Sol* and *Ploughshares*, and have been collected in *The Woman in Red*. Among the awards she has received are a fellowship in poetry from the National Endowment for the Arts and a Fulbright-Hayes Fellowship to Iceland.

RODGER KAMENETZ has published several books of poetry, most recently *The Missing Jew: New and Selected Poems* and *Stuck*. His prose works include *Terra Infirma* and *The Jew in the Lotus*. He has received a National Endowment for the Arts award in literature as well as grants from the Nathan Cummings Foundation and the Louisiana Division of the Arts.

JULIE KANE has published three collections of poetry: *The Bartender Poems, Body and Soul*, and *Two into One*. She was awarded the George Bennett Fellowship in Writing at Phillips Exeter Academy and won first place in *Mademoiselle* magazine's College Poetry Competition.

RICHARD KATROVAS has published four books: *Green Dragons, Snug Harbor, The Public Mirror*, and *The Book of Complaints*. His poems, translations, essays, reviews, and fiction appear frequently in journals and anthologies.

SYBIL KEIN is a poet and playwright with expertise in Louisiana's Creole French dialects. She has lectured on the literary use of Creole at the Sorbonne in Paris, where she was named Chercheur Associé of the Centre d'Etudes Afro-Américaines. She is the author of *Gombo People, Delta Dancer,* and *The Myth of New Orleans in Literature.* Her most recent work is *An American South.*

DAVID KIRBY won the Brittingham Prize in poetry for *Saving the Young Men of Vienna.* He has also published *Mark Strand and the Poet's Place in Contemporary Culture,* a critical study, and for children, *The Cows Are Going to Paris* (with Allen Woodman).

YUSEF KOMUNYAKAA won the 1994 Pulitzer Prize and the Kingsley Tufts Award for his book *Neon Vernacular.* He also received the 1994 William Faulkner Prize (Université de Rennes). He teaches creative writing at Indiana University in Bloomington.

PINKIE GORDON LANE served as Louisiana state poet laureate from 1989 to 1992. She is the author of four volumes of poetry, the latest of which is *Girl at the Window.* She is active on the poetry reading and lecture circuits throughout this country and several African countries.

MARTHA McFERREN has published four books of poetry: *Delusions of a Popular Mind, Get Me Out Of Here!, Contours for Ritual,* and *Women in Cars.* She has been awarded a fellowship in literature by the Louisiana State Arts Council, a Yaddo fellowship, and a fellowship in creative writing from the National Endowment for the Arts. She has also won the Deep South Writers Conference competition and the Marianne Moore Poetry Prize. She lives with her husband Dennis Wall in New Orleans.

LEO LUKE MARCELLO has received Shearman fellowships as well as prizes for his poetry from the Catholic University of America and the Deep South Writers Conference. His books include *The Secret Proximity of*

Everywhere, Blackrobe's Love Letters, and *Nothing Grows in One Place Forever.*

BEVERLY MATHERNE has published three bilingual collections of poetry, most recently *La Grande Pointe.* Her work has appeared in *Two Worlds Walking, Kansas Quarterly, Squaw Review, Great River Review,* and elsewhere. She recently won the national poetry competition at the "Writing Today" conference in Birmingham, Alabama. She is on the writing faculty at Northern Michigan University in Marquette.

DAVID MIDDLETON has published several books of poems, including *Reliquiae, Under the Linden Tree, The Burning Fields,* and *As Far As Light Remains.* He also has edited *Mind and Blood: The Collected Poems of John Finlay.* Currently he serves as poetry editor for *The Classical Outlook.*

WILLIAM MILLS has published three collections of poems, a volume of literary criticism, a novel, and two collections of short stories. In addition, he provided both text and photographs for *Bears and Men: A Gathering* and *The Arkansas: An American River.* His books of poetry are *Watch for the Fox, Stained Glass,* and *The Meaning of Coyotes.* He is a frequent lecturer and reader in this country and abroad.

KAY MURPHY has served as associate director of the writing program at the New Orleans Center for Creative Arts. She has published her poems in *Black Warrior Review, Seneca Review, Tendril, Poetry, New York Quarterly,* and *St. Andrews Review.* One of her essays is included in *From the Heartlands: Photos and Essays from the Midwest* by Wendell Berry, et al.

STELLA NESANOVICH has collected her poems in several chapbooks and published them in numerous journals and anthologies, including *Immortelles: Poems on Life and Death by New Southern Poets, Maple Leaf Rag II,* and *Houston Poetry Fest Anthology 1993.* She serves as poetry and fiction editor of the *Louisiana English Journal.*

SUE OWEN, who teaches at Louisiana State University in Baton Rouge, has had her poems appear in *Harvard Magazine,* the *Iowa Review,* the *Na-*

tion, the *Southern Review*, and elsewhere. She has also published three books of poems: *My Doomsday Sampler, Nursery Rhymes for the Dead*, and *The Book of Winter*. For the last she won an Ohio State University Press prize. She has given readings at universities and PENB Clubs in Moscow, Warsaw, Budapest, and Prague.

GAIL J. PECK has published her work in *Carolina Quarterly, Mississippi Review, The Malahat Review, High Plains Literary Review*, and Deep South Writers Conference chapbooks. Her own chapbook *New River* won the Harperprints Chapbook Competition.

WYATT PRUNTY has published several collections of poems, including *Domestic of the Outer Banks; The Times Between; What Women Know, What Men Believe; Balance as Belief;* and *Run of the House*. His *"Fallen from the Symboled World": Precedents for the New Formalism* is a study of contemporary poetry. He founded and directs the Sewanee Writers Conference held annually at the University of the South.

LISA RHOADES has had poems published in *Poetry East, Abraxas, Poet Lore, Oxford Magazine*, and the anthology *Heart of the Flower*. She has held a poetry fellowship at the University of Wisconsin's Institute for Creative Writing in Madison. Currently she's studying nursing at New York University.

CAROLYN RICAPITO has published a chapbook, *Destinations*, and her poems have appeared in *Louisiana Literature, New Delta Review*, and *Exquisite Corpse*. She teaches poetry in the Arts in Education Program of the Baton Rouge Arts Council, in addition to pursuing her interests in drawing and painting.

SHERYL ST. GERMAIN has been awarded a National Endowment for the Arts fellowship, the Dobie-Paisano Fellowship, and the Ki Davis Award from the Aspen Writers Foundation. Her books include *Going Home, The Mask of Medusa*, and *Making Bread at Midnight*, the last of which was published with a grant from the Texas Council on the Arts. Her most recent collection is *How Heavy the Breath of God*.

KALAMU YA SALAAM was named the Louisiana State Literature Fellow for 1995. Author of eight books of poetry, he is also editor of *Word Up: Black Poetry of the 80's from the Deep South*. His latest book is *Cosmic Deputy*, and his latest recording is *My Story, My Song* for "The Spoken Word" on WRKF, Baton Rouge.

MARTHA SERPAS has published her work in various journals, including *Southern Poetry Review* and *Tar River Poetry*. Recently she has been a student of religion and literature at Yale Divinity School. She also serves as a consultant on the teaching of writing in elementary schools.

LEWIS P. SIMPSON is the author of several influential works of literary history, including *The Brazen Face of History: Studies in the Literary Consciousness in America, The Dispossessed Garden: Pastoral and History in Southern Literature*, and *The Fable of the Southern Writer*. A native of West Texas, he resides in Baton Rouge, where he is Boyd Professor and William A. Read Professor of English emeritus at Louisiana State University. There he also has served as an editor of the *Southern Review* since the inception of its new series in 1965.

DAVE SMITH has published more than a dozen books of poetry, fiction, and criticism. His most recent collections of poems are *Fate's Kite, Night Pleasures*, and *Cuba Night*. He has held fellowships from the Lyndhurst Foundation, the Guggenheim Foundation, the National Endowment for the Arts, and the American Academy and Institute for Arts and Letters. He is coeditor of the *Southern Review* and Boyd Professor of English at Louisiana State University in Baton Rouge.

KATHERINE SONIAT received the 1984 Camden Poetry Prize from the Walt Whitman Center for the Arts for her first collection of poetry, *Notes of Departure*. Her poems are also collected in *Cracking Eggs, Winter Toys*, and *A Shared Life*. The last book was selected for a Virginia Prize for Poetry and went on to win an Edwin Ford Piper Award from the University of Iowa Press.

Lindon Stall has published in the *Anglican Theological Review, The Classical Outlook,* the *Southern Review,* the *Compass,* and other journals. His poems have also been collected in a chapbook, *Responsoria.*

Donald E. Stanford has published three volumes of poetry: *New England Earth, The Traveler,* and *The Cartesian Lawmaker.* Other of his books include *Revolution and Convention in Modern Poetry,* a two-volume edition of the letters of Robert Bridges, and the Yale edition of the poetry of Edward Taylor. He has served as an editor of the *Southern Review* since the inception of its new series in 1965.

Elizabeth Thomas has published poems in *Crazyhorse, West Branch, Outerbridge, Mississippi Review, Willow Spring,* and *Quarterly West.* Her work has been anthologized in *The Pushcart Prize Anthology IX, Woman Poet,* and *The South,* and collected in the chapbook *The House on the Moon.*

David Tillinghast has published *"Women Hoping for Rain" and Other Poems.* In addition, his poetry, fiction, and nonfiction have appeared in *Ploughshares, Virginia Quarterly Review,* the *Southern Review, Texas Review, Wisconsin Review, Poet Lore,* and elsewhere.

Lisa van der Linden, a native of the Crescent City, earned a master of fine arts degree at the University of New Orleans. Her poems in this anthology are her first published work.

Bernice Larson Webb has published numerous poems and articles, as well as a few short stories and one-act plays. She is the author of several collections of poems, including *Beware of Ostriches, Spider Web,* and most recently *Mating Dance.* Her several books include *The Basketball Man,* a biography. For twenty years she served as editor of the journal *Louisiana Poets.*

Gail White, who edits poetry for the *Piedmont Literary Review,* has published four chapbooks of her own. Her work has also appeared in the *Formalist, Sparrow, Verse,* and other journals.

DARA WIER has served as president of the Associated Writing Programs and as a policy panelist for the National Endowment for the Arts. Her books include *Blue for the Plough, The 8-Step Grapevine, All You Have in Common, Blood, Hook and Eye,* and *The Book of Knowledge.* She has received fellowships from the Guggenheim Foundation and the National Endowment for the Arts.

JOHN WOOD is a poet, essayist, and photography scholar. His book *In Primary Light* was the winner of the 1993 Iowa Poetry Prize, and *The Scenic Daguerreotype* was named the "Outstanding Book of the Year" by the American Photographic Historical Society. His essays have appeared in the *Southern Review, American History,* and the *Chronicle of Higher Education.*

AHMOS ZU-BOLTON II has received fellowships in poetry from the National Endowment for the Arts, the Louisiana Division of the Arts, and the Texas Commission for the Arts and Humanities. His work appears in several anthologies, including *Black Southern Voices* and *Mississippi Writers.* He served as director of the eighth annual National Festival of Black Storytellers.